THE PRACTICAL ART OF
BONSAI

THE PRACTICAL ART OF
BONSAI

JOHN HANBY

THE CROWOOD PRESS

First published in 2022 by
The Crowood Press Ltd
Ramsbury, Marlborough
Wiltshire SN8 2HR

enquiries@crowood.com

www.crowood.com

British Library Cataloguing-in-Publication Data
A catalogue record for this book is available from the British Library.

ISBN 978 1 78500 985 3

Cover images
Front cover: *Sageretia theezans* from the private collection of John Hanby.
Back cover: *Taxus cuspidate*, Juniper chinensis, *Acer palmatum* air layer, Korean Hornbeam (*Carpinus coreana*).

Frontispiece
This maple was in my collection for many years and is seen here showing off its autumn colours. The tree was awarded a prize for its amazing flared root base by Mr Daizo Iwasaki at one of the Ginkgo Bonsai Exhibitions in Belgium.

Typeset by Kelly-Anne Levey
Printed and bound in India by Parksons Graphics

CONTENTS

INTRODUCTION

It's hard to believe that I started my bonsai journey more than thirty years ago. Just like you, I was fascinated by the idea of having a miniature version of a full-size forest tree growing in a pot on my windowsill. There was definitely something magical or mystical about this concept and my curiosity was aroused. I had no idea what I was letting myself in for or how it would change and shape the rest of my life. I joke with my students on a beginner's class that just like cigarettes, bonsai should come with a warning note, 'this product can seriously damage your wealth!'; but when I think of the pleasure, enjoyment and satisfaction this hobby has given me, the people and trees I have been fortunate to meet, this product is priceless.

I had tried some seeds but that was a disaster, not one green shoot appeared. Next came a mail-order bonsai, which, the label informed me, was a Japanese temple tree. Unfortunately, this tree did not survive for long, but now I realize I was trying to keep an outdoor tree alive in a totally inappropriate indoor environment. I was determined not to give up and, subsequently, acquired a juniper that I did manage to keep alive for many years, despite its early existence being, again, mistakenly confined to indoors. I suppose my early attempts were not so much thwarted by bad advice but by no real sound advice at all! So, if you are in the same predicament that I was in, I hope that you will find some of the early chapters in this book really useful. The first two chapters should help you in the

Miniaturizing and growing a tree in a small pot just captures the imagination.

acquisition of your tree, whilst the practicalities of keeping it alive and healthy are discussed in Chapters 4 and 5, depending on whether it is an indoor or an outdoor tree.

A Bonding with Nature

Our fast-paced lives today are dominated by the high-tech industrialized civilizations we are a part of. The idea of a slow-paced, gentle, rural environment seems to have all

Outdoor bonsai thriving and brightening up the garden but close enough to the house to be enjoyed from within.

but disappeared. Somewhat surprisingly, the amount of leisure time we have does seem to be increasing and there is a prevailing trend to want to escape to the countryside. The interest in gardening is also becoming more popular with large garden-centres extremely busy in the summer months and more gardening programmes being shown on television. Bonsai allows us to take this connection with nature to another, much closer, level.

To develop a bonsai, you need to harness nature, to work with nature in order to achieve a desired goal or shape. Some of the tasks involved in shaping your bonsai will result in you having to go over every branch of the tree on a regular basis. You will get to know your tree intimately; you will understand and bond with your tree. The transformation is immediately satisfying when you create a bonsai out of a piece of raw material, but then it becomes even more rewarding when you see the tree back-budding and evolving appropriately because of your intervention. Chapters 7 and 8 on branch development should help you in your partnership with nature to build up the structure of your tree and then refine it further.

In my other life, before bonsai, I was a chartered surveyor with my own estate agency business. As my interest in the hobby grew, I found that working on one of my trees was so engrossing it was the only time I could truly forget about work and any other ongoing problems. In addition to this therapeutic quality, you will find that, like most pastimes connected with nature and gardening, bonsai is spiritually uplifting. It will lead you through the seasons, there is always something to enjoy and something to look forward to. Throughout this book I have tried to refer to seasons of the year rather than months in order to make it easier for you to appreciate the timing of tasks. My bonsai experiences are centred around Yorkshire, England, in a temperate climate. Using this information, you will have to adapt the advice given to coincide with the season and climate in your particular location.

Time

Planning your life now will generally involve thoughts and discussions around today, tomorrow, next week and, inevitably, next month. When you start making plans for your bonsai, suddenly you are talking about next year or the year after; days and weeks are replaced by growing seasons. Your concept of time takes on a whole new perspective. Maybe it's not such a bad thing that nature is trying to slow the pace of your life down and instil in you a greater sense of patience. This might sound daunting and long-winded, but it is surprising how quickly time goes by and how your trees will change. People say you should enjoy the bonsai journey and not just the arrival at the destination. But you don't want to be stuck at a station, time is precious and it is much nicer to arrive within a reasonable period of time. I have viewed the collections of some enthusiasts after twenty years' involvement in the hobby and their trees have changed little. As a bonsai teacher, I do find this frustrating when I know how much a tree can be improved in just five years. However, if they have enjoyed their trees and had much pleasure from the hobby over the years, who am I to criticize? But people can lose interest in the hobby and become disappointed or frustrated when they are failing to make progress. Most of my students are excellent bonsai technicians and they just seek some input from me to point them in the right direction to take their trees to the next level. For things to change and to move in the right direction, it is important that you are performing the right tasks at the right time. Mr Takeo Kawabe, the bonsai master I studied with in Belgium, instilled in me the principles of 'watch and wait'. Leave your trees alone, let them grow, watch them and wait until the time is right to intervene again to carry out the next task. Enthusiasts often do too much to their trees in too short a time and the trees suffer as a result. They need time to recover.

I hope the information in this book will inspire you and encourage you to make those correct decisions on your trees to develop them and, ultimately, refine them to a higher level. The many case studies and examples will show you just how much your trees can progress in a relatively short space of time.

If you buy an expensive specimen bonsai from Japan, you are basically paying for time; for the fact that someone in Japan may already have invested thirty years in the tree's development. It is much more satisfying if you have created the same sort of bonsai yourself from a garden bush or stump. It can also be a good investment in that your tree may now be considerably more valuable, whilst the enjoyment and pleasure you have experienced is, again, priceless.

One of my privet stumps pictured in June 2002 having been retrieved from a hedge.

The same privet stump pictured in July 2017 after fifteen years of bonsai cultivation.

Two old bonsai in part of a display garden I created for one of my Newstead Bonsai Extravaganzas.

A Living Work of Art

There is a strong bias in this book towards the horticultural aspect of bonsai, after all this is the information you need to keep your tree alive and healthy. If you have a sick tree, you can do nothing but wait for it to recover. If you have a strong, healthy tree, then you can utilize the other horticultural techniques explained to develop and refine your tree. But we must not forget that bonsai should really be viewed as a work of art and respected accordingly. Each created bonsai represents a vision of the artist and his or her interpretation of how a tree can look, whether it be a perfect miniaturized replica of a stately, full-grown tree or a more conceptual 'living sculpture'. The aura surrounding

a well-executed bonsai is much more at home in a gallery situation than it is in a horticultural tent. Having mastered the horticultural side of bonsai, I hope that the principles and philosophies of art in bonsai, explained in Chapter 9, will enable you to successfully combine the two and further improve your trees.

With other art forms there is a beginning and a definite end. Once painted, a picture can be framed and hung on the wall, a statue can be mounted and placed for all to admire. With bonsai there is a beginning but there is no ending – it has that extra dimension, life itself! In creating your work of art, you have to allow for its future development, its seasonal changes and plan ahead to carry out the work required to eventually achieve the image that you have in your mind. Then you have to improve and maintain that image.

Something to Think About

I was once interviewed for a bonsai magazine and was asked where my knowledge and inspiration had come from. I told the interviewer that I had learned from my mentors, my students and my mistakes. (If my students read this they will be trying to charge me for the privilege!) The fact that you are working with a natural, living plant does mean, regrettably, that fatalities will occur. Sometimes the cause is down to nature and beyond your control. Sometimes it is down to you, making mistakes, perhaps expecting too much from your tree, bad repotting or inadequate watering. Over the past thirty years I have lost trees, I have made mistakes, but through my school, and now this book, in the ensuing chapters I hope you can learn from my mistakes and keep your trees alive and healthy. Don't get too disheartened if you do lose a tree, but try to learn from the experience and move forward. I remember a story about a bonsai enthusiast once talking to John Naka, a famous bonsai pioneer in America. The despondent student was telling John about some of his trees struggling and not looking good. It was perhaps even more frustrating to visit John's nursery and see all his benches full of trees looking so strong and healthy. John turned around and quietly enlightened the student, 'It's not that I don't have any sick or dead trees, I just don't put them on display'.

What you will be surprised to find is that the problem will, inevitably, become totally reversed. When we talk about 'our trees' I suppose we are guilty of being a bit blasé. We are, after all, very much a servant to our trees. We take care of their every whim and no expense will be spared in ensuring that they have the best possible conditions and husbandry to survive and flourish. In this scenario they are capable of outliving us by many years, even hundreds of years! For the time they are in our possession, we really are no more than custodians, humble servants. As your collection develops, it is certainly worthwhile trying to encourage your children or grandchildren to take an interest, if only to ensure that your beloved trees' progress will survive through future generations.

It would be great if a bonsai came with a 'log book' that chartered its history and previous owners. Some trees I have sold have passed through my hands several times and

How my *Euonymus* looked when I acquired it after it had two owners. It started life in Sheffield and then went to the Isle of Man.

just from what I know of them they have quite a story to tell. Trees suffer adversity, they are restyled, they are given a new pot or different planting angle. A pictorial record would be really interesting and invaluable, especially when some bonsai, like in Japan, are hundreds of years old. Chapter 10 will help you to put your trees and your collection into perspective with advice on starting your own bonsai records.

The tree when I exhibited it in Belgium in 2016, after which it appeared in an international bonsai magazine.

CHAPTER 1

BONSAI ORIGINS

A Brief History

China

Contrary to what most people would think, it is generally accepted that bonsai originated in China, rather than in Japan. Ancient manuscripts and paintings confirm that artistic pot plants were being grown in China as early as AD700.

The Chinese have a great practical love for flowers and plants, whilst their spiritual heritage has strong links between humans and nature. There was something mystical about nature and especially the mountains. Being able to recreate a mountain landscape in their own garden would have been highly regarded.

When we go for a walk in the hills and mountains today we capture the scenery with an image on our phone or camera.

I used the raft planting technique to create this mountain scene as a demonstration for a bonsai club.

The same *Juniperus communis* as raw material prior to the demonstration.

Many homes in Japan have a tokonoma – a niche or alcove where they can mount a display. Entire books have been devoted to the selection and arrangement of the display elements.

It is so easy for us to access this and to share the image with family and friends. In those early years the Chinese would use rocks, mosses and plants to try to recreate a landscape they had been inspired by, in their own garden. This would have been a valuable source of contemplation and meditation, which could be shared with visitors.

Chinese bonsai are often associated with the distinctive 'S'-shaped trunk and the separate foliage pads/clouds. I was once told by a friend with strong Chinese connections that the separate foliage clouds represented the steps to heaven. The curves in the trunk were put in place because they believed evil spirits could not change direction, so this would stop them pursuing you on your upward journey.

Japan

Buddhist monks are credited with spreading the idea of miniature landscapes and trees into Japan from around the twelfth century. When you think of Zen Buddhism, the idea of peaceful contemplation and intuitive meditation, there is again a strong link between humans and their natural surroundings. Ancient traditions, and this strong spiritual bond between humans and nature, no doubt played its part in the early development of the bonsai art.

Over the years, as bonsai gained popularity, the trees that were created in Japan became much more refined, especially in the last century. The Japanese took bonsai to a whole new level and have become renowned throughout the world for this art form. They still seem to be able to combine an appreciation of the natural tree image, whilst creating trees that sometimes appear to be almost too perfect.

The magnificent bonsai created in Japan are the inspiration for many of the trees created in the rest of the world today. In my early bonsai days, I had been teaching the hobby quite successfully for several years and considered myself to be reasonably competent. Then I came into contact with enthusiasts in Europe who had been taught by the Japanese. It was like starting out all over again!

A thriving business has evolved, in both China and Japan, exporting bonsai trees, pots and accessories to many countries.

The West

The first significant introduction of bonsai to the Western World appears to have been towards the end of the nineteenth century. Aristocrats and Victorian plant-hunters were searching the world for new and interesting artefacts

Satsuki azalea bonsai on display at my own Newstead nursery. Every two years, for one weekend my main greenhouse was transformed into an amazing exhibition hall.

and plants; they returned from the east with tales of minia-ture trees artistically twisted and contorted.

The intervention of two world wars in the twentieth century certainly seems to have slowed down the interest in, and the development of, a bonsai hobby. However, in the USA it gained in popularity after World War II, probably due to soldiers being stationed in Japan.

In the 1960s and 1970s there was certainly a thirst for knowledge and more people were beginning to dabble with creating miniature trees. My own personal bonsai story was sparked in the 1980s and it's surprising how many of my contemporaries started their bonsai journeys at around the same time.

Today

Bonsai today is a thriving and rewarding hobby enjoyed by people across the world. Most countries have a network of bonsai clubs and groups where people can come together locally to share knowledge or to show off their latest crea-tion. You may be surprised to find that there is a group of likeminded enthusiasts local to you or within reasonable travelling distance. Many local and regional horticultural shows now incorporate a bonsai section or display. Local, regional and national bonsai exhibitions are held regularly

in most countries. These shows are a great source of inspi-ration and pleasure. International bonsai exhibitions are also held annually or biennially; for example, the Kokufu-ten in Japan, the Trophy show in Belgium and the US National exhibition in America. These shows attract exhibi-tors and visitors from across the world.

There are many established bonsai nurseries where you can pick up supplies locally and perhaps source your next tree (*see* the stockists listed in the Further Information sec-tion at the end of the book). Of course, we now also have the internet and, like everything else we need to survive on this planet, everything bonsai can be purchased online.

Dispelling the Myths

Definition

Most people are familiar with the concept of bonsai. They see it basically as a full-size tree that somehow has been miniaturized and is kept in a tiny pot. Having encountered the full-size version in the wild, there is this fascination and something magical about how the tree can be kept small and survive in such a limited amount of soil. They see bonsai appearing regularly as a background item in films and television dramas, most noticeably in *The Karate Kid*. Some people even think it is cruel; that the trees are starved, strangled with wire and wedged into a pot that is ten sizes too small. Speak to the partner of a bonsai enthusiast and, if reincarnation is on offer, you will find that they will all be coming back as a bonsai; the care, love and devotion lavished on these small trees is beyond reproach.

A common error is for people to think that bonsai is a special type of tree. So, just like we have an oak and a pine tree, they think we have a bonsai tree. The literal translation of bonsai is 'a tree in a tray'. So the definition is more about the concept rather than a specific type of tree.

If a bonsai tree were removed from its pot, planted back in the ground and allowed to grow unchecked then it would revert back to being a full size natural tree. It would take many years for the tree to reach its normal natural height and girth. This would be influenced by the local climate, soil, and how favourable the growing conditions are.

Age

Bonsai are quite capable of living as long as many of the trees growing naturally in the wild. In Japan, some bonsai have well-documented histories revealing that they are over 500 years old. They are handed down through the generations just like family heirlooms that we are familiar with in the West.

On one of my classes with Japanese bonsai master Takeo Kawabe, at the bonsai school in Belgium, we were discussing a juniper that had originally been collected off the mountains in Spain. After discussions between the master and some Spanish students in the class, they estimated its age to be in the region of 500 to 600 years. When you think what has happened in the world whilst this small tree has been growing, it makes you truly appreciate what you are working on, what you have in your hands; it is a humbling experience.

So, age can be important but don't get carried away with it. Some people will exaggerate the age of their trees, especially if they are trying to sell it to you. It is often a

Yamadori Bonsai

This Japanese term describes bonsai that are collected from the wild. Many of the famous trees in Japan, and some of the top-quality bonsai in Europe, were created from material dug up off the mountains. I have heard stories of people hiring helicopters to bring trees home from the higher mountain regions. It is not uncommon for a yamadori collector to be seen hurtling down a mountainside on skis with the upper branches and foliage of a tree sticking out of his backpack.

The attraction of this material is that it already is an old tree with matured bark, aged deadwood and twisted/contorted branches but remains small. It has been dwarfed naturally by the harshness of its location – avalanches, cold temperatures, the weight of snow and strong winds. It takes skill and experience to be able to remove an old tree from its mountainous home and accustom it to life in a container whilst keeping it alive and healthy.

You should always seek permission before removing a tree from land that does not belong to you. In some cases, for example National Parks, the fines imposed for unauthorized removal of plants and trees can be very high.

For and against

The practice has been going on for centuries and will be encountered in some form by every bonsai enthusiast. I do not advocate wholesale indiscriminate removal and vandalism of the countryside: please note the need to obtain permission and the possibility of heavy fines being applied.

Self-sown seedlings often grow like weeds in some areas, and their removal can be welcomed by some landowners. The Forestry Commission will often let bonsai collectors access specific sites to remove unwanted young material on the edges of plantations.

Every year, people clear shrubs and trees from their gardens to make way for home or garden improvements, depositing them in skips or on bonfires. Some of this material has excellent bonsai potential – you just have to be in the right place at the right time. It can be a similar situation when local authorities are clearing roundabouts and other areas of public land: one bonsai enthusiast found excellent old pine material on a walk in the Scottish highlands. He faced a lot of red tape to remove these trees. The next time he went up the grouse moor had been set on fire and all the trees had been totally destroyed.

The yamadori bonsai collector is more interested in saving trees and plant material, looking after it and taking it to a whole new level.

Like most things, there are arguments for and against. You will no doubt make up your own mind, but it is my duty to present to you what is a valuable part of the hobby.

guess anyway; trees don't generally come with a birth certificate. Just because a tree is old does not mean that it is automatically a good tree. I have seen people pay high prices for yamadori raw material that had very limited potential to make good bonsai. The best basic advice is to buy a tree because you really like it.

Size

Bonsai come in all shapes and sizes. There are many named size classifications to have come out of Japan and these have given rise to much discussion and conflict. Basically, it doesn't really affect you unless you intend to exhibit your tree. In which case, the rules adopted by the exhibiting body may determine specific sizes for each class and, ultimately, which section your tree will be placed in.

What it does mean is that you can have a reasonable bonsai collection in whatever size space you have available, be it a balcony or a large garden.

Before I acquired a small hydraulic lift, if I wanted to work on some of my trees I had to make sure my helpers brought them into the studio before they went home. Generally speaking, the older you get, the smaller your trees tend to become, at least in theory!

This larch was originally collected from the Alps. It has been wired and styled and is just coming into leaf.

A display of shohin bonsai at my Newstead Bonsai Exhibition in 2010.

Common Size Classifications and their Approximate Dimensions

Mame	5–15cm (2–6in)	Palm-size bonsai.
Shohin	13–20cm (5–8in)	You can hold it comfortably in one hand.
Medium size	25–75cm (10–30in)	Within this section, you may come across 'Kifu' and 'Chuhin' classifications.
Large size	75–120cm (30–48in)	These are often divided into two-person, three-person or four-person trees, which is the number of people required to move the tree from one place to another.
Patio bonsai	Over 120cm (48in)	These larger trees are more like patio trees sitting in an almost permanent position due to the effort required just to move them.

Unlike some commodities, the size of the bonsai has no significant bearing on price or value. For example, you could have a large, partly trained tree of reasonable appearance worth a few hundred pounds and a specimen shohin bonsai of really good quality worth a few thousand pounds.

A typical Chinese elm bonsai tree sold as an indoor variety and the first direct contact many people have with bonsai.

Your Bonsai Origins

How Did You Arrive Here?

Maybe you have that fascination with these miniature trees we mentioned earlier and are just eager to find out more information. Could this be a new hobby you want to get involved in? Many people are introduced to bonsai because they have received one as a gift, often as a Christmas or birthday present. In this modern age, if people want something, they tend to go out and buy it, so it becomes increasingly difficult to buy a gift for people who literally have everything they need. It's that magical and mythical aura that surrounds bonsai that makes it an ideal gift; most people are really happy to receive one.

Unfortunately, many people then have to confess that they have killed a bonsai, largely due to bad advice or not being given any correct instructions in the first place – a problem this book hopes to try to resolve.

For some people, bonsai is a natural progression from a love of nature or horticulture. People who like gardening will inevitably dabble with bonsai at some time. The interest may be generated by something so simple as self-seeded saplings that they find in their garden or whilst out walking.

How you arrived here and what you are looking for can have a big impact on how far you go and where you finish up with this intriguing hobby.

Future Considerations

If you have received a bonsai tree as a gift, you may simply want to acquire sufficient information to be able to keep the tree alive and in reasonable shape. In the vast majority of cases, the bonsai gift tends to be an indoor tree (see Chapter 4). People want to enjoy their gift as much as possible and, therefore, it is kept in a prominent position within the home.

Indoor or Outdoor Bonsai

Most of the trees sold as indoor bonsai in the West are imported from China. In their natural environment they are sub-tropical or tropical species, which grow naturally outside. When you keep this tree inside your home, you are basically trying to recreate its natural environment artificially. If you live in a more tropical climate, then you would be able to grow these species as outdoor bonsai.

Outdoor bonsai are the same species that you see growing naturally all around you. Just like their full-size counterparts they need the seasons, the changes in temperature, the winter dormancy and so on. They include the classic bonsai species – pines, junipers, maples – and are the trees grown by the vast majority of bonsai enthusiasts.

If you come from a strong gardening background, or start to show more interest in the hobby, then you will soon realize that the outdoor varieties (see Chapter 5) are the more popular trees, offering much greater diversification and potential.

The design of your house and garden could play an important part in what type of bonsai you grow. A flat with a small balcony may dictate that you stick to indoor bonsai or just have a few small outdoor trees. If you have a young family demanding a lawn on which to play, the siting of your outdoor bonsai display could be crucial to avoid damage from footballs and other unidentified flying objects.

The local climate could have a strong bearing on the types of trees you can grow successfully. If your garden is exposed and subject to strong, cold winds, then maples are unlikely to flourish. If your garden is heavily shaded by neighbouring trees, then you may have to consider species

Your outdoor bonsai display can become an important feature in your garden. This may then lead to the acquisition of additional features, such as the Japanese water-basin and watering-can.

that will thrive in this type of environment. Explore your local area and see what types of trees are growing naturally in the neighbourhood. If you can make contact with local bonsai enthusiasts, they will soon be happy to tell you which trees grow well and which ones tend to struggle.

How much time and money do you want to invest in the hobby? One of the good things about bonsai is that it is very adaptable in terms of these two constraints. As you will see in later chapters, you can create your own bonsai from very inexpensive material, virtually nothing. Alternatively, you may wish to invest money in an established bonsai that has been imported from Japan, an object of beauty to give immediate pleasure; basically you are buying time. If you have a demanding job and a busy lifestyle, then you may only be able to devote a small amount of time to your hobby. This could dictate that you only have a few manageable trees. The more time you have, the more trees you can have and the more effort you can put into working and refining your trees. For many retired people who suddenly have a lot of free time, bonsai as a hobby can be life enhancing.

Once you get more involved with the hobby, you may find that you discover your own niche. You may be drawn towards the powerful, classical, evergreen bonsai subjects, like pines and junipers. I have had some students with a bonsai collection centred entirely around the deciduous maples and the many different varieties available. Another student loved flowering trees, so she tried to build a collection that gave her flowers all the year round: as one tree faded, another one would just have the flower buds opening.

You may be drawn to a certain size of tree. Some enthusiasts have collections based entirely on smaller size mame and shohin bonsai.

It may seem that there is much to consider, but the hobby is so adaptable it can give you great pleasure and satisfaction, whilst accommodating your lifestyle, budget and location.

It is hard to resist a Satsuki azalea bonsai in full flower, especially when you get different-coloured flowers on the same tree.

RIGHT: With strong summer growth this bonsai is reverting back to being a bush, but is a subject that ticks all the boxes for many enthusiasts. Maples are generally popular but the red new growth of this Deshojo variety shows just how stunning the tree looks in spring when it is completely crimson.

BELOW: After a short pruning session, order is restored, and this natural looking forest planting can be truly enjoyed. Forest plantings enable us to replicate a dramatic landscape in miniature. Furthermore, we only put this group together a few years ago with relatively young, inexpensive material.

CHAPTER 2

STARTING OUT
Your First Bonsai

Sources of Bonsai Material

Garden Centre

If you have not received your first bonsai as a gift, then it looks like you will just have to go out and buy one yourself. Most of the larger garden centres will nearly always have a small selection of indoor bonsai for sale, together with a few sundries, such as food, wire and pots.

Look over the trees on offer and make your selection carefully. You will be drawn to one that you particularly like, but the main thing is to check its condition. Are the leaves clean and unblemished? Brown tips could suggest that the tree has been kept too wet. If leaves are shrivelled, brittle or dry then the tree may have dried out at some point. If the leaves are sticky then the tree could be subject to an aphid attack. The problem is that usually the staff at the garden centre have no experience of looking after bonsai, so they are treated just the same as any other plant. They are prone to being under- or over-watered, as mentioned above. Long, unpruned, spindly extensions of shoots could mean that the tree has been for sale for quite some time, making

A selection of good Chinese elms for sale – unblemished leaves, bright colour, evidence of new emerging growth and moist compost.

Autumn on the bonsai nursery – a time when some trees can look sad and some can look spectacular.

correct watering even more difficult and leading to a weakening of the tree.

Sadly, many people have been put off the hobby because they think they have killed their tree, when in truth the tree was probably dying when they bought it.

Specialist Bonsai Nursery

If you really want to improve your chances of buying a strong, healthy tree, have a better selection and be able to get some sound practical advice, you can't beat a visit to your nearest specialist bonsai nursery. The reputable specialist nursery will have a good selection of both indoor and outdoor trees in various price ranges. You should be able to find reasonably priced starter material and better-looking, more developed trees to satisfy whatever budget you have in mind.

Just remember, whenever you have limited knowledge and experience, it is better to start with cheaper basic material. Whilst it would be disappointing if you lost any of this material, it would not be a financial disaster. The material will have served a valuable purpose if you know where you went wrong and can avoid making the same mistake in the future. Once you have mastered the basics, and find that you can confidently keep your trees alive

and healthy, then you can return and treat yourself to that more expensive, amazing bonsai that you fell in love with on the very first visit.

The bonsai nursery owner is usually also an enthusiast, so you will usually find him or her eager to pass on tips and advice, especially when a successful and satisfied customer is more likely to return. You should ask them if they know how old the tree is, when it was last repotted, has it been fertilized on a regular basis and for any advice specific to your tree's species.

Just take note of where the tree is growing in the nursery relative to the time of year and climate. For example, if it is winter and the tree is protected under glass in the nursery, it could be a severe shock if you take it home and leave it outside overnight in an exposed position. Look over the tree and check for any signs of infestation. Are the leaves clean and free from any obvious fungal problems? Is the tree secure in the pot? If it is very loose, then this could indicate a problem with the roots. Are there weeds growing in the pot depriving the tree of food and water? Is the compost loose and fresh, which could indicate that the tree has been recently repotted? If it is solid, then the tree may have been in the pot a long time and watering could be difficult, as most of it will just run off the surface. After much deliberation and discussion, you should finally be ready to leave with a good choice and your first serious bonsai. Now the fun really starts!

The Internet

If you are someone who prefers to do all their shopping from the comfort of the living room, gazing at a computer, then purchasing bonsai is not a problem. Most specialist bonsai nurseries have their own website that incorporates an online shop where you can buy trees, tools and accessories. In fact, some bonsai suppliers only sell online and do not have a nursery you can visit. Where possible, check any reviews or awards available, to ensure that you are dealing with a reputable supplier who has a track record of performing well and in satisfying customers. There is always a risk in sending living plant material through the post and in a fragile ceramic bonsai pot. You are totally dependent on the supplier watering the tree well and packaging it, so that it does not dry out or get thrown about and broken.

One of the main problems is that you are buying from a photograph. You don't know for sure how recent the picture is. Even when you zoom in, it is difficult to make a sound judgement on the tree's health and if there are any obvious problems. Photographs of trees can be deceiving, so there is always the gamble that when it arrives, it could easily be better or worse than you were hoping for.

I once had a lady on a class with a pine that she had bought off the internet but as soon as I saw it I had to break the news to her that it was, in fact, a spruce.

Creating Your Own Bonsai

Seeds

Many aspiring bonsai enthusiasts will have been given a bonsai seed kit as a gift to get them started in the hobby. The box usually contains some seed, a small bag of compost, a tiny ceramic bonsai pot, maybe a bit of wire and some very basic instructions. I have to be honest, I have often referred to this product as 'consai'. They tend to give the impression that all you have to do is plant the seed, water it and 'hey presto' you will finish up with an amazing bonsai. To make matters worse, they often have a picture on the front of the box of a magnificent old specimen bonsai tree from Japan that was probably collected from the wild and not grown from seed anyway. I stand in awe of

It could take six to twelve months to get your bonsai seed to this stage.

some of my students who have turned up on workshops with amazing trees that they have grown from seeds that were planted over thirty years ago. It is very rewarding but takes amazing patience and there are other ways of getting a much quicker result, which we will discuss in due course.

It could take several years before you can actually start doing any bonsai work on your seeds, especially with conifers, and it is hard to maintain your enthusiasm for the hobby when you have nothing to show for it. Seeds are perhaps something you can come back to or try when you have other trees and ongoing projects to occupy your interest and satisfy your bonsai needs.

One possible shortcut with seedlings is self-seeded plants that you may come across in your own garden or whilst out walking. This can be a useful source of starter material to get you going at minimal expense. Being young plants they should be easy to transplant with plenty of fibrous root. Reduce the long, thick, tap root as much as you can to encourage more fibrous roots and to enable you to, ultimately, be able to plant it in a shallow bonsai pot. You should always seek permission from whoever owns the land before attempting to remove any plant material.

Self-seeded field maple and hawthorn growing at the side of a path.

The long, thick, tap root is reduced, leaving a shallower, fibrous, root system nearer the base of the tree.

Cuttings

Using cuttings will generally gain time on using seeds, will enable you to select the mother plant and is a good source of free material from your existing stock or garden. It is particularly useful if you are creating young material from which to make a forest planting because, if the cuttings are all taken from the same parent plant, they will all be true to type.

I generally take softwood and semi-ripe cuttings from late spring and throughout the summer. The subject of the instructions here is a blackthorn but the same principles apply to most of the broadleaved trees and shrubs we use for bonsai.

The cuttings can be placed in a seed tray or plant pot, ensuring that they are not touching each other. If you have a propagator or can provide under-soil heating, this will improve your chances of success. The compost needs to be kept damp and the atmosphere humid. I have bent wires to support a large polythene bag over the tray to create a tent-like mini-greenhouse. A polythene bag could also be placed over the plant pot and secured with an elastic band.

Taking softwood and semi-ripe cuttings

Step 1: Remove a long shoot from the new season's growth.

Step 2: Cut at a leaf node (joint) and also remove the soft growing tip.

Step 3: Remove all but two leaves and the cutting can then be dipped in a rooting compound or gel.

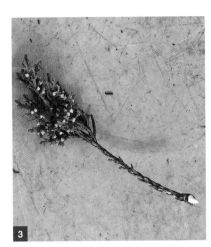

Taking evergreen cuttings

Step 1: Select a side shoot that is approximately 7.5–10cm (3–4in) in length.

Step 2: Tear it away from the trunk so that it comes off with a small heel.

Step 3: Trim the heel and remove the lower foliage from the cutting.

You can use a seed potting compost but I have also had good results with a 50/50 mixture of perlite and grit. The cuttings will often root in as little as three weeks.

For evergreen cuttings, such as junipers, I take a heel cutting.

The juniper cuttings can then also be dipped in a rooting compound and placed in a seed tray, as detailed for softwood and semi-ripe cuttings. I have had good success with junipers using neat akadama (Japanese bonsai soil) in the tray. Without bottom heat, these cuttings can take much longer to root, sometimes months.

Ground Layering

You will find that many trees will layer in the ground naturally. Low branches may droop or get pushed down so that they come in contact with, or are partially buried by, soil. The buried branch is then capable of producing roots that eventually can sustain the branch as an independent plant and allow it to be removed from the parent tree. You can exploit this by selecting low branches of a tree you wish to layer and pegging them down in the soil to hold it firm, whilst it has chance to create roots. Occasionally, you can check the layer by tugging gently at the plant to test for resistance due to it having formed its own roots, which are now holding it in the soil.

Once it has sufficient roots, you can sever it from the parent plant and pot it up. It can then be placed in a greenhouse or sheltered spot to recover and grow on. You could also try layering the shoot directly over a pot rather than in

These three-year-old *Juniperus ittogawa* cuttings are ideal for grafting, or growing on in the ground with some initial trunk bending.

the ground. Removal would then just involve severing the branch from the parent and the tree would already be established in the pot. You just have to make sure that the branch is held securely in position whilst rooting takes place.

Sometimes you will find layering occurs naturally with nursery stock in a plant pot. I have often pruned buried low branches away from a trunk and found that they have roots attached. Prunings to be discarded can sometimes be a source of free new material.

A pyracantha just developing its flower buds and with a low branch on the left that we could remove.

A closer inspection reveals that having been buried, the branch has produced its own roots. It can be removed and potted up separately – two plants for the price of one!

Air Layering

This is another technique for creating roots on a stem but this time the operation is carried out above ground. You need to try to start this up as early as you can in the season, so that you will be in a position to remove the rooted section and have it potted up before winter. However, the tree needs to be growing strongly when you do the work, so it will usually be late spring or early summer.

If air layers fail, it can often be because the moss has either been too wet or has dried out completely. This is something that you can check when you are periodically looking for signs of roots.

Air Layering

Step 1: A large *Acer palmatum* garden tree capable of providing us with potentially two bonsai. A light trim allows us to look inside.

Step 2: Inside there is a long, straight trunk section that has no taper or side branches. If possible, try to select a point on the trunk where there is a leaf node, as this will increase your chances of producing roots.

Air Layering (cont'd)

Step 3: Completely ring bark the trunk at this point, removing the bark and all the cambium layer below. The depth of the ring should be equal to the diameter of the trunk in this area. This work was carried out on 22 April 2020.

Step 4: Apply a rooting powder or gel to the stripped area. A small, wet brush will be required for the powdered form. It is a good idea to start with fresh powder or gel each growing season.

Step 5: Wrap a ball of wet sphagnum moss (the same as you use for hanging baskets) around the ring bark and then wrap the whole thing with some clear plastic. This can be tightly secured with bonsai wire or tape.

Step 6: Cover this with some black plastic from an old compost sack. This will absorb more heat and also help stop the sun drying the sphagnum moss. From time to time, you can check to see if there are roots by removing the outer wrapping without disturbing the layer itself.

Step 7: 8 August 2020 – the tree has been allowed to grow unchecked with no pruning whatsoever.

Step 8: Try to be patient and not remove the layer when you see the first white roots, these are very fragile and brittle. Wait until you get plenty of strong healthy brown roots like these.

Step 9: The top is pruned back to the basic tree shape of the air layer. This will take pressure off the relatively small amount of new roots we now have.

Air Layering (cont'd)

Step 10: Carefully remove the layer by cutting the branch just below the new rootball, taking care not to damage the fragile roots.

Step 11: It can then be potted up. I have had good results using a compost mix of two parts akadama and one part chopped sphagnum moss. We have no roots to anchor the tree, so we improvise with a wooden block.

Step 12: The base of the original tree is also shaped to form another bonsai. The remaining trunk of the air layer will be reduced and hollowed-out to give the image of a much older tree.

The task described here is the complete ring bark method. Some books advocate leaving a narrow bridge of bark intact but I think the danger here is that the tree can try to survive on the bridge rather than producing new roots.

Another method is the tourniquet technique, where you twist a wire deeply into the bark to interrupt the flow of sap. If you try this, use two shorter wires rather than one long wire, so that you can twist the wire from both sides. Twisting from one side can lead to a gap at the point from where you are twisting.

I have successfully air layered many deciduous species, as well as juniper, pine, hemlock and *Taxus*. I tried using the different methods on different varieties but I am afraid the results were inconclusive. Generally speaking, the complete ring bark method would seem to be the most reliable and successful technique.

When you compare air layering with seeds in one season, you can have a sizeable trunk potted up whilst the seedling is barely showing above the ground. This useful technique can also enable you to create another tree out of a large branch that you might have been going to cut off anyway. Sometimes it can be used to overcome faults in the lower trunk by allowing you to create a new root system in a more favourable place.

Plant Material from the Garden

In carrying out your general gardening duties, you will inevitably have come across trees that have seeded themselves and invaded your borders. Up until now you will have frowned at these intruders, treated them like weeds and somewhat aggressively dumped them in the waste bin.

With bonsai now implanted in your mind, your whole attitude changes. The uninvited guests are now welcomed as a potential source of free new material. Now you need to carefully extract it with as much fibrous root as possible, remove any strong, downward-growing tap root and lovingly pot it up in a plant pot. At this stage, you could use a standard container compost from your local garden centre.

The best time to do this work is, ideally, in spring just when you see the buds starting to move or change colour. However, sometimes you may have to act quickly if you need the area clearing now or maybe it's a plant in a friend's garden that needs moving.

If the tree has a lot of top growth relative to the amount of roots, trim the branches back to restore the balance and to take pressure off the roots whilst it re-establishes itself. Don't forget to water it well once you have completed the potting-up process. For the rest of the growing season it is best to just leave the tree alone and let it recover. Place it in a sheltered spot and water as necessary, not letting it dry out completely.

Up until now we have generally been talking about growing up our material from small, humble beginnings – seeds, cuttings, young seedlings and layering. Another option we have is to bring larger material down. Somewhere in your garden you may have an old shrub or tree that has seen better days, become straggly or overgrown and generally outgrown its use. Ideally, you are looking for something with an interesting trunk, mature bark and, if possible, low branches that could be utilized. The main thing is the trunk, because we are going to re-grow most of the branches. It will be like starting out with a large seedling in a pot but one that already has age, character and a large trunk. It gives you the opportunity to create an impressive, old-looking bonsai in a relatively short period of time.

The same rules apply in terms of trying to extract it with as much fibrous root as possible, potting it in a suitable container, removing a lot of the top growth and giving it the correct aftercare. The problem here is that this tree may have been in the ground a long time. Its roots may be substantial and deep, and often it does not want to be removed without a fight. The trowel and fork you were removing the seedling with earlier may have to be replaced with spades, a pick axe, serious pruning shears, a bow saw and even a chain saw. This can be quite a challenge but the rewards can be amazing.

Collecting from the Wild

Trees collected from the wild are referred to as yamadori trees, a topic we touched on briefly in Chapter 1. Generally speaking, material collected from the higher mountain ranges of the world tend to be of superior quality and character due to the harshness and extremes of the climate experienced by the dwarfed trees struggling to survive.

I dug this privet out of a hedge in November 1999; the hedge was about 3m (10ft) high. The photo was taken in January 2001. The tree has survived and started to grow branches.

The same tree exhibited in Belgium in 2016. Later that year it appeared on the front cover of an international bonsai magazine that is translated into six languages and sold worldwide.

This type of material is something you may become more interested in once you have more experience and if bonsai becomes one of your major hobbies. Collecting this material is beyond most of us and often left to people who live in the areas themselves, can source the material and know how to successfully remove and transplant it. We generally have to rely on buying it from a third party, such as a specialist bonsai nursery. Because of the difficulties involved in obtaining this material, the time/care needed to establish it in a pot and its understandable desirability, don't be surprised to find it carries a high price tag. It, therefore, really is imperative to know when the tree was collected and if it is fully established in its container. The age of the tree and the trauma of the transplant mean there is a high mortality rate. Beware of collected trees in massive, oversized containers because, sooner or later, you will have to reduce that rootball to fit in a more appropriate, small bonsai pot – a task that could prove fatal.

At the lower altitudes of the UK, it is still possible to find good and interesting material. Many good pines and larch have been collected in Scotland. *Taxus*, blackthorn and hawthorn have been collected from parts of Wales and areas bordering the Lake District. Apart from a harsh climate, some of this material may also have been kept small by animals grazing it. You do need to get permission from whoever owns the land before you start digging or there could be serious consequences, including arrest. Try contacting large land-owning organizations, such as the

This juniper was originally styled by a snow plough in Tesco's car park. My student Roy was granted permission to remove it.

Two years later and together we gave the tree its first styling.

After another three years, the tree has a new pot and lots of fresh foliage as it recovers and develops well.

Forestry Commission or the National Trust. They will often allow small groups or individuals to access certain areas of land on specified dates to dig and collect material. They may well be happy to see the removal of self-seeded weed-like growths of small trees on the edges of managed plantations.

As bonsai gradually takes over your mind (and this will happen, trust me), you will become more observant in your everyday routine journeys. Home-owners ripping out hedges, local authority workers clearing roundabouts – those old shrubs and trees destined for the skip or bonfire, can all make excellent bonsai.

Early spring or when the tree is dormant are the best times to lift the tree. If you try and lift the tree when it is in full leaf or growing strongly, this could be too much of a shock for the roots and the tree could collapse. However, sometimes timing is out of your control. I once had to lift a large garden maple in July when the tree was in full leaf and growing strongly. I cut all the branches back and removed 90 per cent of the leaves. Within six weeks the tree rewarded me by budding all over and producing another crop of leaves. I had taken the pressure off the roots and at the same time encouraged it to bud and leaf out again.

In all cases, you are trying to lift the tree or shrub with as much fibrous root close to the trunk as possible. The heavier roots can be cut back or removed, especially the ones growing downwards, provided you have sufficient fibrous roots remaining. These small roots are the feeder roots that will enable the tree to survive and make it easier for you to ultimately plant it in a smaller bonsai pot.

If circumstances allow, sometimes people will undercut the tree in the ground all around and underneath, where possible, but then leave it in situ for another year. Basically, they are cutting through the longer heavier roots to encourage the tree to then back-bud and produce finer roots nearer the trunk. This should then make the job of lifting, one or even two years later, easier and with a greater chance of success.

A large foliage mass will have to be reduced, partly to enable you to be able to transport the tree home, but also to take pressure off the roots. Try to remove branches you don't think you will need in styling the tree. Long branches can all be cut back to try to keep a tree shape, but one that produces a smaller canopy. Help on styling and selecting branches will be given in later chapters.

If possible, try to spray the rootball with water and then seal it in a polythene bag, so that you can keep it moist until you get home to pot the tree up. It is important not to let the roots dry out completely whilst they are exposed, as this could prove fatal.

Once home, pot the tree up as soon as you can into a suitable container, just large enough to take the rootball comfortably. More larger roots can be removed but it will always depend on having enough fibrous roots remaining. Use a good, free-draining compost: 50 per cent peat/50 per cent horticultural grit is a good basic compost. Bonsai composts will be discussed in greater detail in Chapter 6.

Water the tree well and place it in a sheltered spot. If it is a conifer, try to mist spray the foliage every day to take some pressure off the roots. Just let the tree grow and recover for as long as it takes; this could be one or two growing seasons.

Nursery Stock Raw Material

When I first started doing bonsai, I could tell you what suitable bonsai raw material was available in every nursery or garden centre within a 10-mile radius of home. I never went past one without stopping, always on the lookout for that next great tree. In those days, the older nurseries and garden centres would always have battered, old and damaged material that they couldn't sell to the gardener but was great for us. It would have older bark and the damage or neglect suddenly became character. It also meant it was cheaper too.

Sadly, most large, modern garden-centres are more like supermarkets and shopping centres. Plant sections are often smaller and fresh young plants arrive almost daily off the back of supplier lorries. They simply want to buy in-season plants and sell them all. They don't want to produce their own or have plants to look after, especially over the winter.

Working with nursery stock is a great way to learn bonsai. It's probably the nearest we get to creating 'instant' bonsai. I use this term very loosely, it takes many years to create a good bonsai, but this can be a good start. That initial transformation can be dramatic and, unlike most other sources, you can immediately have something satisfying to look at and care for.

In the first instance, you are looking for a plant that has a stem resembling a trunk that you can then arrange the foliage around to look like a small tree. I will discuss more about how to start turning your plant in to a bonsai in Chapter 3.

Beginners' Bonsai Class – Trees from Basic Nursery Stock

This selection of trees was all created by students attending one of my beginners' classes. Most of them had no experience of practical bonsai work and they had never wired a tree before.

I helped with the styling, both before and after the wiring. My helpers were on hand to guide the students through the wiring process, if they were experiencing difficulties.

In each sequence, the first picture shows the basic tree purchased as nursery stock. The second picture shows the tree with branches selected and ready for wiring. The final picture shows the tree given its first styling after the wiring was completed.

After a few hours work, each student had the basis of a tree that they could develop further and refine but from which they could get immediate pleasure and satisfaction.

Spruce. Originally looking like a small Christmas tree, it now has the image of a large mature forest tree.

Juniperus chinensis 'Blaauws' variety. Live branches have been made into deadwood, bent downwards and linked with a shari of stripped bark on the trunk.

Juniperus communis 'Green Carpet'. Wiring and manipulation of the branches has enabled us to create a bonsai in the semi-cascade style.

CHAPTER 3

NEXT STEPS
Initial Styling

How Big a Tree Do You Want?

When I ask a student this question, as we study his favourite tree, it usually produces a petrified look of anguish, whilst his fellow classmates are smiling as one. If you purchase an established bonsai with a well-defined shape growing in a ceramic bonsai pot, then the size it is now is more or less how it will stay. It will have seasonal growth expansion for health and refinement but, ultimately, the canopy will be pruned back to keep it in proportion to the trunk. The trunk itself will thicken slightly over a period of time but this will be a very slow process due to the confinement in the pot.

When I used to trade at craft fairs and agricultural shows, people would look at buying a small, indoor bonsai and ask how long before it grows to be like the taller one standing next to it? The answer is never. If you want a taller, bigger tree, save up and buy that one. Don't expect the small one you can afford now to grow into what you really want.

If you are creating the bonsai yourself, using one of the methods outlined in Chapter 2, then you do have more of a say on the aspect of size. Grow your material on to get the trunk as thick as you want it and then you can start to select and develop the branches. The quickest way to achieve this is by planting your aspiring bonsai material in the ground. I have been told on numerous occasions that one year in the ground is worth four years in a pot.

The lawn in front of my bungalow became my growing-on bed, but you could utilize spaces in your garden borders.

Encourage the material to grow strongly with regular feeding and watering, as required, whilst keeping weeds under control. Lower branches can be allowed to grow unchecked to help fatten the trunk and give you options for using some of them when it comes to designing your tree. A leader at the top of the tree can also be allowed to extend but should be replaced with another shoot from time to time to promote taper in the trunk. When planting young material in the ground, you can add some interesting movement in the trunk using bonsai wire or you can insert a garden cane in the soil and wrap the thin, flexible trunk around the cane. Keeping the main leader attached to the cane will help it grow upwards and encourage it to build up the trunk more quickly. In Japan, particularly with conifers, they sometimes leave this initial wire on the tree, allowing the bark to completely grow over it. It can add character and girth to the trunk and becomes totally embedded inside the tree. As the desired shape/size of the tree begins to emerge, keep side branches near the proposed apex under control, as we don't want overly thick branches in this area. Just be wary that if you leave a deciduous tree in the ground for too many years, the fibrous roots could extend away from the trunk making it difficult to lift and get back into a small container. You could consider growing in the ground for a few years, then two years in a pot and then back in the ground. All the time you can be working on building your tree's image and improving the branch structure, whilst still fattening the trunk.

If you don't have any spare ground available, you can grow your trees on in plant pots or a training box. Larger, shallower containers are better than deep pots because we want to encourage the roots to grow outwards rather than downwards. This helps to prepare the tree for its future life in a shallow bonsai pot and also encourages the base of the trunk to flare outwards, which is desirable and more natural-looking.

If you are potting on from one pot into a larger pot for more growth, don't make the step up in size too big. This could result in a lot of compost with no root activity, which could then remain wet, deteriorate and cause problems within the pot from blocked drainage holes and root rot.

Once you are happy with the basic form of your tree in terms of trunk size and any skeleton branches, you can cut the tree back to a basic, triangular shape, lift it and pot it on in a box or training pot ready for further development. The ongoing training of branches and twigs are discussed in more detail in Chapters 7 and 8.

Basic Design Considerations

Once you become interested in bonsai, you will start to see trees growing naturally in the wild in a whole new light. You will begin to appreciate form and design, ramification and character; you will even become critical of faults, telling Mother Nature where she went wrong! You will begin to understand trees. The fundamental principles underlying the basis of designing a tree will become more obvious. Trees generally flare out at the base and have strong exposed roots gripping the soil for support. The trunk will show good, even taper from the base to the apex. The lower branches will be the heaviest in size and character and, depending on the age of the tree, will start to slope downwards. They are the oldest branches and the longest, as their tips of foliage continually stretch outwards from under the canopy desperately seeking light. The branches nearer the apex will be thinner and simply project outwards and upwards. These branches are younger; access to light is much easier and less restricted. This ongoing growth and reaching for light produces the broad-canopied, triangular shape you associate with a parkland tree.

The broad canopies of mature trees growing in the grounds of Chatsworth House where conditions are good and open space is plentiful.

The existing front of this large Kiyohime maple bonsai created from a garden tree.

As the tree has developed, I am now thinking the opposite side might be the new front with its broader canopy, more impressive root base and the view of the hollow trunk.

Bonsai is basically an illusion. You are trying to create in miniature something that looks like a full-size tree growing in the wild. It's these natural basics of design that must be in the back of your mind when you are studying your material and deciding where to start. The more of these traits you can incorporate, the better your finished image will look.

When considering the design of your tree, you will eventually have to decide on a front. This is the side from which you will view the tree, so it will determine the tree's position in its bonsai pot. It should be more open, so that you are looking into the tree. The first branch, often called the character branch, can set the tone for the rest of the tree and is perhaps the most important branch. From our observations of nature above, it is supposed to be the oldest branch and should, therefore, be the thickest branch. Ideally, the lowest two branches should be angled towards you almost like they are greeting you. A branch at the back of the tree will give you depth and provide a backdrop for the trunk. The remaining branches can be arranged around the trunk as you progress up the tree.

If there is movement in the trunk, this should be visible from the front. We don't want the trunk bowing inwards, as you look at it, nor do you want it 'pigeon-breasted' bulging towards you. Don't get too obsessed with the front; it is not to be set in stone. You will find that as the tree develops, sometimes a different view emerges, often when you least expect it, suggesting a new, better front for the tree. If you have purchased an established bonsai, don't assume that the existing front is automatically the best one. When the time comes to repot, look around the tree and consider possible alternative viewing angles; you might be surprised at what you see.

When trying to find the tree in your piece of raw material, it is probably easier if you try to find a trunk line rather than the front. You start at the base of the tree and work your way up, trying to extend your trunk line in to a side branch that will give you a natural flow, taper and some interesting movement. A good piece of material may have several options for the trunk line, so then it is a case of trying to pick the best one or the one that pleases you most. Once you have established this line and selected useable side branches that fit in with the design, everything else will ultimately be removed. A more in-depth look at design and bonsai aesthetics can be found in Chapter 9.

Left: A Japanese black pine from my collection and an excellent example of the formal, upright style.

Japanese Bonsai Styles

One of the early translations of information on bonsai to come out of Japan was the identification of certain styles of tree. Each style is generally determined by the nature and character of the trunk. Whilst you may not be familiar with these styles of bonsai, you will probably be able to relate them to full-size trees and landscapes that you have seen in the wild. Having some basic knowledge of these various styles and categories of tree can be really helpful when you are trying to create your own tree or planting out a piece of raw material. When you are examining the trunk line and possibilities in your raw material, as we detailed earlier, if you can then relate this to an established bonsai style it might just make it easier to see and to create a natural-looking tree image. The various styles and their characteristics are illustrated with the Japanese name for the style shown in brackets.

Formal Upright (*Chokkan*)

As its name suggests, this tree is very formal with a perfectly straight trunk having excellent taper and a good, even distribution of branches around the trunk. The lowest branches are the heaviest and the thickness of each branch decreases as they rise up the trunk. The first two branches should open from the trunk as if they are greeting you, whilst the third branch should be towards the back giving you depth. This could be the parkland tree you find in the grounds of a stately home with plenty of sheltered space, so there is no competition for light and no severe weather to bend the trunk; it is literally left to grow onwards and upwards. It could also relate to trees found in a forest situation, but here there is much more competition for light and limited space available, so the growth is forced upwards. These trees would have the same straight, tapering trunk but the branches would be nearer the trunk making a very tall, narrow canopy. Good examples of this would be pine trees and the mighty sequoias.

Left: A *Juniperus ittogawa* as it was imported from Japan, ready for wiring/styling but with a nice informal trunk showing gentle movement and good taper.

The long branch on the right of this old cedar is a perfect counterbalance to the slope of the trunk, creating a perfect, stable image.

You can almost sense the wind blowing through this purple beech forest. The trunks have tried to grow straight but have been forced to bend to the right. Some branches are making a half-hearted attempt to grow into the wind. Really pleased with this image, as the picture was taken immediately after the group had been created from garden-centre stock.

Informal Upright (*Moyogi*)

This will be the style that most of your trees will probably belong to and the one where you would place any trees that don't specifically fit into any other recognized style. The trunk will have reasonable taper, but there will be evidence of curves and movement. There will be greater leeway in the number and distribution of branches. In the wild, trees like this are growing in a position that is a bit more exposed to the wind and weather, which has resulted in the movement in the trunk. They may also be growing nearer other trees or in uneven terrain, which has caused them to adapt their shape as they reach for greater light and better conditions.

Slanting Style (*Shakan*)

The main line of the trunk is generally straight and with a definite slant. The triangular canopy is calm and natural with branches all around the trunk. In the natural environment, you may find this type of tree growing on sloping ground or perhaps trying to grow away from some natural obstruction. A windswept tree is also likely to have a slanting trunk but the branches will prevail more to one side and the movement in them will be more dynamic.

Windswept (*Fukinagashi*)

This style represents trees growing in more extreme, exposed locations on high ground or along the coastline. The direction of the wind will be obvious, with the trunk and branches all being forced to grow towards the leeward side. There may be evidence of decay and deadwood if the tree has taken a severe battering. The more severe the conditions, the more dynamic the movement in the branches. With a successful bonsai created in this style, the viewer can almost sense the wind rushing through the tree. They are often planted on slabs or rocks to enhance that natural landscape feeling.

The picture of this shohin *Juniperus ittogawa* was taken shortly after styling. The deadwood in the trunk and upper branches suggests a harsh environment, with the live foliage growing downwards and outwards for light and protection.

Semi-Cascade (*Han-Kengai*)

With this style, the movement in the trunk is generally to the side and slightly downwards. The movement and slope in the trunk is quite gentle. Branches are arranged almost in tiers, supporting neat clouds of foliage. In the wild, you would find this tree growing out of embankments or low-lying cliffs and perhaps overhanging water.

Full Cascade (*Kengai*)

The obvious difference between this style and all other bonsai styles is that here the main movement in the trunk is definitely downwards. The downward movement is much more dramatic than the semi-cascade style and is more likened to a plunging waterfall. When creating this style, the trunk should move from front to back, as well as from side to side, to create a more three-dimensional image. The side branches will, again, be arranged in tiers with clouds of foliage. This tree would be found growing probably in higher, more extreme mountainous conditions, perhaps growing out of a sheer rock face or in a small pocket of soil.

Juniperus chinensis recently wired and styled with a plunging downward trunk line. The strong pot shape gives the tree stability, both aesthetically and in real time, by not been easily blown off the display bench.

We would probably have to remove the lower branches on the right and the thin, hanging-down branches on the left to make this Chinese elm a classic broom-style tree.

This *Juniperus sargentii* from Japan was probably collected off the mountains. The dramatic twists and turns in the trunk are made even more dramatic by being a combination of live veins and deadwood.

For most of the year, the interest in this *Forsythia* bonsai is in the dramatic appearance of its exposed roots over the Ibigawa volcanic rock. For now let's just enjoy the flowers!

Broom Style (*Hokidachi*)

So-called because the tree resembles the top of an upturned Japanese broom. The trunk is straight with a reasonable root spread and branches generally radiate evenly outwards from the top of the trunk. The canopy is rounded with branches getting progressively thinner and resulting in many fine twigs. This style is mainly appropriate with deciduous trees, as the tree often looks at its best in its winter image, where the refined branch structure is clearly visible. It is generally planted in shallow, oval or rectangular pots. It is the tree style you will often see growing in local parks and urban streets.

Literati (*Bunjingi*)

This style is named after the 'literati' who were scholars considered to be the elite of Japanese society and is likened to their calligraphic work. The trunk of this tree is thin and tapering, often with dynamic movement. The interest is generally more in the trunk than in the foliage, which is often just a small triangle sufficient to keep the tree alive. Its charm and beauty is in its simplicity. It is often planted in round pots. You might find this tree growing in extreme weather conditions in the mountains or a lone survivor on some desolate moor. Sometimes Scots pines growing at the side of major roads can illustrate this literati style.

Root Over Rock (*Sekijoju*)

The roots are trained over the rock from an early age, so that they follow its contours and almost become part of it. The Japanese achieve this by planting the whole rock and securely tied tree in the ground for several years. It is allowed to grow strongly and as the roots swell, they will merge with the rock. The tree is styled by matching the canopy with the roots and rock, which now together represent the trunk. On moors and dales where rocky outcrops dominate the landscape, you will often find exposed tree roots amazingly growing over large, solid stones.

Root On Rock (*Ishitsuki*)

This differs from the previous style in that the tree is actually planted on to a rock. Soil is introduced on the rock and the tree is transplanted from its existing container into this new pocket of soil. In effect, we are creating a landscape whether it be an island rising out of the sea or the craggy summit in a range of mountains or hills.

Three *Juniperus ittogawa* planted on a piece of rock from China. This picture was taken immediately after its creation at an evening demonstration for the North and East Lincolnshire Bonsai society.

The trunk on this Satsuki azalea has been replaced by exposed roots but still it manages to retain its dignity and poise with its last flush of summer flowers.

This *Taxus cuspidata* was created on one of my demonstration days. Originally, the whole tree had live bark and the deadwood to the right was actually the live apex. The tree was tilted to the right and what was the lowest, left-hand branch, became the new apex.

Driftwood Style (*Sharimiki*)

Most of the trunk will be shown as deadwood and the bark will have been stripped off. You may have to create this tree in stages to alleviate too much stress and you have to ensure that you leave adequate live veins to connect the roots to the remaining foliage. This style is most commonly used with conifers but you may come across a deciduous tree where it is appropriate. The deadwood is bleached white and preserved with lime sulphur, which creates the dramatic stark white effect. This can be toned down to create a more natural-looking grey appearance for deciduous trees. This style may be representative of decaying ancient trees or those found in the very harshest environments nature can throw at us.

Exposed Root Style (*Neagari*)

The roots can be quite dramatically exposed and replace the lower section of the trunk. It can almost appear as though the tree is trying to walk out of the pot! Sometimes you may come across trees in exposed locations, where wind and rain have eroded and washed or blown away the soil around the base of the tree, leaving the roots exposed and now above ground level.

Twin Trunk (*Sokan*)

Two trunks growing very close together. The trees may share the same base and root system or they may be two individual trees. Normally one tree is likely to dominate the other. If the second tree is considerably smaller, then this is often referred to as a 'mother and daughter' arrangement. In the wild, the smaller tree would normally be the younger tree, so ideally the lowest branch in the composition should emanate from this tree. The overall canopy will be designed as if it were just one tree. This is a common arrangement you will come across when walking in the countryside.

These two red Deshojo maples work well together, sharing similar characteristics, and the composition has a natural plausible feel about it.

This Japanese larch group had just been repotted and the rocks repositioned to form an escarpment. Covering the surface with moss would bring about an amazing transformation.

A Japanese maple clump in all its autumn glory. The mature grey bark tells you immediately that this is a really old tree.

Forest Planting (*Yose-Ue*)

Individual trees are brought together and arranged to create a natural-looking forest planting. They are generally planted in a shallow container or on a thin slab to enhance that feeling of a landscape. When the general public visit a bonsai exhibition, this is often their favourite creation because they can relate it to woodlands they have seen and it gives them the complete sense of a landscape in miniature. It's like looking across a field at a small, wooded copse. Relatively young seedlings can be brought together in a forest planting to create an illusion of something much older.

Clump Style (*Kabudachi*)

There may be three trunks or there could be enough to make it like a small forest, but with this style, the trunks all emanate from the same base and, therefore, share the same root system. Similar rules apply to this style as with the creation of a twin trunk or forest planting. Once again they are generally planted in shallow containers. It is a style more commonly found in deciduous trees and is a style you will often encounter naturally when walking in the countryside.

Juniperus chinensis 'Blaauws' variety in the raft style. You can just make out the original trunks we laid down on the surface of the soil.

Raft Style – Straight (*Ikadabuki*) or Sinuous (*Netsunanari*)

If you come across this happening in nature, it can be quite dramatic. Sometimes, when a tree falls over and is laid on the ground, part of the root system can remain connected and survive. Over a period of time the branches will continue to grow upwards and eventually appear like trunks or separate trees in their own right, albeit that they are still connected by the original trunk at ground level. We can replicate this by laying our raw material on its side, cutting off downward-facing branches and wiring upwards the remaining branches to simulate a small forest. We encourage new roots to grow out of the laid down trunk, so that we can eventually cut off the original raw material rootball and then plant the raft in a shallow container.

A collected silver birch seedling growing strongly in July, but the three trunks are long with no movement or taper and are out-scaling the trunk.

Pruned back, I now have a more compact trunk from which we can build a tree. This will encourage all the buds you can see and other dormant buds to grow, giving us more design choices. The wire is no longer required.

Initial Pruning

Deciduous Trees

When you start to initiate a design in a piece of raw material, the first pruning can be very dramatic. Sometimes, almost all the existing branches and foliage may need to be removed. It is highly unlikely that you will find a piece of raw material with a perfect trunk and all the branches you need growing in the correct place on the trunk and exactly the right thickness they need to be. Unless the tree is a high-quality specimen bonsai, it is also likely that most established bonsai you may acquire will still need work in sorting out the basic branch structure.

Established shrubs from the local garden centre or dug out of your garden may offer good potential but, once again, some drastic action may be required to initiate a style in your material. Up until now these shrubs will have been allowed to grow freely, their only task being to provide an abundance of flowers, seasonal colour or to fill a space with greenery. Often at this stage, all we can try to do is identify a basic trunk line and remove everything else, unless there are branches we may be able to use. We will then grow new branches where we need them to shape the tree.

I would normally try to carry out this drastic pruning to deciduous trees in late spring/early summer when I can see that the tree is healthy and growing strongly. Once you remove this large amount of growth, all the energy that has been used to produce it has to go somewhere, which results in new buds emerging all over the tree, both extensively and quickly. If your tree is weak and sparse to start with, then it is better to leave any drastic action until after it has recovered and is growing strongly again. Further development of the branches and increasing ramification is discussed in greater depth in Chapters 7 and 8.

Coniferous Trees

Just like with the deciduous tree, it is often the case that when you carry out your initial styling of a conifer, a rather drastic amount of foliage will have to be removed. However, you must now be prepared to adopt a more careful and considered approach. With most conifers, the energy and strength of the tree is in the foliage and its growing tips. Whereas a strong deciduous tree will bounce back if you cut all the foliage away, if you did this with a conifer it is more likely to die, and if it did recover,

A multi-trunk *Escallonia*, but these trunks are so straight with no taper and not at all tree-like.

A privet dug out of a hedge that has grown back very strongly, but those three trunks have no taper whatsoever and just look like sticks.

Grow some more fine branches and twigs on this trunk and already you have something resembling a tree in its winter image.

Now we have the potential to make a very powerful shohin-size bonsai by growing branches and forming a canopy. The large pruning scars and some of the base can be completely hollowed-out to create the image of an ancient, rotting tree.

This *Ligustrum* has been left to grow unchecked. It is unkempt but strong and healthy.

Selecting side branches to give a change of direction produces a pleasing basic form and a trunk line that has movement and taper, with enough existing side branches to create a pleasant tree image.

it will have been considerably weakened. Once you start removing more than two-thirds of the existing foliage, you have to be careful.

The same initial design considerations that we discussed earlier will also apply to conifers. However, it can be a little bit more difficult finding that initial trunk line and branch structure because your basic raw material will often be dense in foliage. Some branches may have to be removed just so that you can see what's happening inside. Remembering that you want thicker branches near the base; thinner branches near the apex can be a big help in deciding which branches you need to remove. You are trying to remove sufficient foliage so that you are left with a trunk line and a skeleton form of branches ready for wiring to create that initial tree shape in whatever style you may have considered appropriate. You are an artist creating an image but you are not starting with a blank canvas or a solid block of wood/metal, you are starting with a natural, living plant. In theory, you are removing everything that doesn't look like a tree. You can also remove any small bits of foliage on the trunk or on parts of branches nearest the trunk, just so it makes it easier for you to apply the wire. (Wiring is discussed later in this chapter.)

Confidence

One of the big problems that stop people moving forward with their bonsai at all stages of development is lack of confidence. When it comes to pruning branches, you only get one chance at it and if you get it wrong, you simply can't stick it back on! With my bonsai classes, apart from giving people information, advice and inspiration, I think the biggest thing they gain is more confidence. It is truly amazing how everyone sees how obvious it is to cut a large branch off their fellow student's tree, but when it comes to their own tree, they suddenly become blind and extremely cautious. Some students will happily walk away, leave their tree in my hands and tell me to just cut off whatever I think is necessary. With other students, I know it will take maybe two years to cut off a certain branch. It has to be suggested gradually and discussed on several occasions before I finally get the go-ahead. And then, lo and behold, amazingly their tree looks so much better. We could have been here two years ago. By showing you so many sequence pruning examples throughout this book, I want to try to give you greater confidence to be a little bit more adventurous with your own trees.

Example One: *Juniperus chinensis*

Step 1: A relatively small *Juniperus chinensis* but so many options. At this angle, all the lower branches could be removed to leave a long, tapering trunk, with just foliage at the top to create a literati-style bonsai.

Step 2: A cascading tree could be created using just the first low branch and the rest of the trunk could be shortened and made into deadwood.

Step 3: Two options here: we could just use the upward-pointing branch and amend the angle slightly to create an informal tree, or we could just use the long, downward-hanging branch to create a full cascade.

Step 4: Decision made! It's a good piece of material that gives you so many viable options. Ultimately, you have to decide either which is the best or which you prefer.

Example Two: Nursery spruce

Step 1: A large, bushy spruce with multiple trunks/heavy branches. The very low ones can be removed.

Step 2: There is a poor 'catapult' configuration where the trunk splits. The thinner trunk gives us better taper and useable side branches.

Step 3: A tree begins to emerge from the bush with a tapering trunk, some heavy low branches and thinner upper branches.

Step 4: The planting angle is altered slightly. The long, low branch to the left provides an excellent counterbalance to the general movement of the tree to the right.

Example Three: *Taxus baccata*

Step 1: My student Alan dug this huge *Taxus* out of his garden and brought it to a private class in February 2019. Timing is excellent here, as the work is carried out just before the tree will start growing strongly, which will greatly aid its recovery.

Step 2: I started removing foliage around the edge of the tree just so we could get to look inside.

Step 3: And then I got carried away! It was a case of finding a possible trunk line, leaving some heavier branches lower down and keeping thinner material around the top of the tree.

Step 4: We had to get the tree into a training pot, which meant greatly reducing the rootball and, therefore, I needed to reduce the foliage mass to keep it in balance with the roots and take pressure off the tree.

Step 5: March 2020 and the tree is back in the classroom. Really pleased with the new growth in just twelve months.

Step 6: So once again we can make a selection and the tree is beginning to emerge from the original huge bush. We can now see an impressive tapering trunk, a basic branch structure and some deadwood to camouflage the larger branches we had to cut off.

I spoke earlier about taking care when removing foliage on conifers to get to the wiring stage. Sometimes it may be necessary to remove unwanted foliage in stages to allow the tree time to recover. You need to ensure that you are leaving enough foliage with strong growing tips to keep the tree alive and flourishing. Once it has recovered from the initial 'attack' and started to produce new greenery in the areas where you want it, then you may be able to start taking it back a bit further. Doing this over a period of time also enables you to grow new useable branches in the places where you need them. Once the tree is strong enough and you have sufficient branches for a styling, then you can move to the wiring stage.

Affectionately known as 'The Dragon's Tail', I suspect that this specimen white pine would never have been allowed out of Japan but for the demise of the long branch, which gave rise to its name.

Less than twelve months later and after many hours of wiring. I wired every branch and twig on this tree and the result is really satisfying.

Wiring

Why Do We Apply Wire?

Apart from the confinement in a small pot, wiring is another area where we bonsai enthusiasts are often accused of cruelty. The words contorted, twisted and tortured are often encountered, suggesting pain and suffering. Wiring is a means to an end; in the same way that a gardener would tie a climbing plant to a trellis or a pergola. In each case we are trying to encourage the tree to grow in a certain way or direction, and we are offering support until it gets established. As explained already, you are never going to find a piece of material where every branch is growing in exactly the right position to produce the perfect image of the tree you had in mind. Wiring of a bonsai is likely to be required at every stage of its development. As a young seedling, the trunk planted in the ground is wired to create that initial curving shape with added interest. The thickening main branches will be wired in to place so that they set the basic framework for the whole tree. Developing side branches will then be wired to ensure that they complement the tree's desired design and appearance. Twigs may have to be wired in to place as they continue to regrow to maintain an immaculate image. Some of this work can be achieved by careful selective pruning, especially with deciduous trees: the 'clip and grow' method. In fact, often the better, more natural-looking images are obtained by a combination of the two techniques.

The ultimate aim is to finish up with a specimen bonsai having all the inherent traits of maturity and age, together with a dense, impressive canopy, where every branch and every twig is in exactly the right place but with no wire on the tree whatsoever. A magnificent bonsai at this level can often reduce the viewer to a state of awe, and sometimes tears! To achieve this level, a tree in Japan may have been wired thirty to forty times during its life. Our art form is unlike any other, it has that added dimension of 'life' itself. Nature will pull branches towards the light, encourage them to produce more growth, leaving you having to correct this unruly behaviour with another wiring!

Types of Wire

Aluminium Wire

Anodized aluminium bonsai wire imported from China or Japan is the most commonly used wire and the one you are most likely to come across, both online and in bonsai nurseries. It is soft and relatively easy to apply, whilst its

Aluminium wire is available in lots of different gauges with coils in two weight sizes.

A portable wire caddy is a great way to keep your wire tidy, whilst making it easier to see and select the correct size.

5kg coils of copper wire wrapped as they arrive from Japan. The weight has actually broken this nursery crate!

unobtrusive colour blends in well with branches and foliage. It is also available in a good range of sizes; the thicker the branch you are trying to wire, the larger the gauge of the wire you will need to move and hold the branch in position. At the present time, wire is supplied in sizes from 1mm to 6mm with every half-size in-between. Now 1.2mm and 1.8mm sizes are also available, which extends the range and is a big help when it comes to selecting the correct wire size for the very fine branches. The coils of wire are generally available in 100g and 500g rolls. Beginners will generally buy a few smaller coils in the sizes they need, but once students become seriously interested in bonsai, they quickly construct some form of transportable wire caddy and fill it with a 500g roll of every size.

Copper Wire

Copper wire is not as readily available and coils of imported Japanese copper wire are often sold in 1kg or 5kg rolls, which make it much more expensive, especially when you are trying to put together a reasonable range of sizes. The copper wire has to be annealed to soften it and make it useable. Once you apply it and bend it on your tree, it changes its molecular structure, which then sets it solid. It, therefore, has a much better holding power than the aluminium wire, especially in the thinner gauges. I have not come across any copper wire that performs as efficiently as the Japanese wire. This wire seems to be annealed to just the right degree, so that you have time to apply the softened wire and manipulate the branch before it sets. With other copper wires I have encountered they tend to start setting solid before you get to the end of the branch,

making it difficult and dangerous to apply. Perhaps this is why you tend to come across copper wire being used more in Japan and by bonsai professionals. Many students who have attempted to use copper wire do seem to find it much more difficult to use and, consequently, are happier to stick with the aluminium.

When you are able to accumulate a good selection of Japanese copper wire, it is particularly useful for refinement wiring on mature specimen bonsai. On a tree like this, the main, heavier branches are already set in place, so the extensive detailed wiring required is centred around the many fine twigs and secondary branches. When I wired the white pine pictured earlier under 'Wiring', between 0.5mm and 1.5mm I had eight different wire sizes to choose from. Had I been using aluminium wire, I would only have had 1.0mm, 1.2mm and 1.5mm available. The larger gauges available in aluminium are also available in copper.

Poor Substitutes

A word of warning! I have seen people trying to economize using all sorts of cable, from green plastic-coated garden wire, to steel wire, to plastic-encased electrical cable and copper wire that has not been annealed. These materials are much more difficult to apply, will not provide you with the desired solution and may even cause damage to your tree. If you are unable to acquire the correct materials, you might be better just relying on the 'clip and grow' method.

Wiring Technique

Coniferous Trees

Most of the detailed wiring when we apply wire to almost every branch on the tree is generally carried out on conifers. As you have seen in previous photo sequences, the initial styling starting with a 'bush' involves selecting branches, cleaning out some of the dense foliage and then wiring the trunk/main branches to form the basic skeleton of the tree. As the tree develops and grows more secondary and finer branches, then subsequent wiring becomes more intensive, as all these branches have to be wired too.

Wiring Coniferous Trees

Step 1: To wire the trunk, we must first anchor the wire by pushing it into the soil. We can then coil it evenly around the trunk, trying to make 45-degree angles between the wire and the trunk, whilst carefully threading it in-between any side branches.

Step 2: When you are applying the heavier wire sizes, if you are struggling to manipulate it with your fingers, then try using your jin plier, especially when you get near the end of the wire.

Step 3: Now we can get some movement in the trunk. Caress the wired branch or trunk into position. Roughly bend it and it is prone to snapping! Notice how the arrows mark the points where we have bent the trunk. We are pushing against the wire, which is on the outside of the curve, protecting it from snapping.

Step 4: If you imagine this is a small tree ready for wiring and we are happy with that bit of movement in the trunk. I thought it would be easier to illustrate the technique more clearly in this format rather than trying to show it on an actual tree, where branches and foliage would hide the detail.

Step 5: We always wire branches in pairs, so that the two wires will anchor one another. Select branches as near to equal thickness as possible. Here we have selected the two branches forming a continuation of the trunk. The heavy base of the branches has provided a good anchorage point, whilst the coiling of the wire is the same technique as for the trunk. Excess wire at the tips is cut off.

Step 6: Now we select the next two branches and use a slightly thinner wire. We follow the line of any existing wire, ensuring that the wires don't cross and keeping them tight together. Going around the intervening trunk at least one and a half times will ensure that they are properly anchored.

The heavier the branch you are trying to wire, the thicker the wire you need to apply to the branch. As a general guide, the diameter of the wire will need to be at least 30 per cent of the diameter of the branch. The tree species and the age of the branch may also have a bearing on how supple the branch is, which could further affect your choice of wire size. There is no substitute for experience and, like most things, the more you practise, the better your wiring technique will become and the easier it will be to select the correct wire size. If you are undecided between two possible wire sizes for a particular branch, I would say that in almost every case it will be the larger one that you need. It is

Wiring Coniferous Trees (cont'd)

Step 7: When you bring your wire into a side branch, if you intend to bend the branch downwards, you come over the top of the branch. If you intend to bend the branch upwards, you come underneath it. As before, you are then pushing against the wire when you move the branch.

Step 8: Using the same technique and a thinner wire, we then continue to wire the finer twigs at the end of the branches, trying not to damage the foliage. The letters show the sequence of applying the wire and which branches have been paired together.

Step 9: The remaining branches are wired in the same way. The branch on the left marked B and F only had three shoots at the end, so I extended the wire B into a side shoot, leaving the remaining two shoots to be wired together. This maintains the wiring-in-pairs' approach, ensuring that every branch is adequately anchored.

Step 10: We have been wiring this example as an upright tree but if we lay it down and view it from above, as if it were a branch, the technique is exactly the same. What represented the trunk has now been wired as if it were a branch leading from the main trunk.

very rare I come across a student using a wire that is too heavy, but frequently students use a wire too thin to enable us to move the branch to where we want.

You need to adopt a methodical approach to your work, so start at the bottom, select the two branches you intend to pair and apply your main wire that links them together. Continue with the lowest branch and wire all the remaining shoots and side branches. Move on to the linked branch and do the same, then continue with this procedure all the way up the tree until it is fully wired. You can shape/position the branches/twigs as you progress up the tree.

Many students try to measure a piece of wire for each of two branches they intend to connect. I find it easier and quicker to cut a long piece of wire, apply it to two branches, cut the end and move on to the next branches until it runs out and then I cut another long piece. You will also have less wastage with this technique. You can see the long wire I am using in the photo accompanying Step 6.

When you look at the picture of the finished wired branch, there is a certain neatness about it. No crossing wires, you can still see the underlying structure of the tree and most branches only have one wire on. I have seen some wired trees that look almost like coiled springs, with no bark visible and often that is how they behave with the branch springing back and not holding its intended position.

Sometimes we need additional pull or support on a wired branch, so a guy wire may be introduced and secured to a jin or the rim of a plastic training pot. A turnbuckle can be used, where we need to secure this movement, as a gradual process to reduce the risk of breaking the branch.

Deciduous Trees

With most conifers there is a degree of flexibility in the branches, up to a certain point. When you are struggling to bend a branch that you have just wrapped in 6mm wire, a little voice inside ought to be saying 'should you really be trying to bend this branch?'. By comparison, the branches on deciduous trees are much more brittle and prone to snapping without warning. The 'clip and grow' technique is much more widely used with deciduous trees, but wiring can help with correcting wayward branches and in setting the position of younger branches in the early stages of development.

The principles and technique of applying the wire is basically the same as we set out for coniferous trees. However, I do tend to use a slightly heavier wire size on deciduous trees and I also try to wire with a little bit more looseness. Branches can swell and grow much more quickly with deciduous trees, so the wire can bite in after a relatively short time before the branch has had time to set. The movement we want in these branches is often slight and much less dramatic than with conifers, so a slightly heavier wire does the job well and is easier to apply more loosely.

When Is the Best Time to Wire a Tree?

The tree you are planning to wire should ideally be strong and healthy, as this task can be quite a stressful operation. If your tree is sick or having problems, it is better to let it recover, regain its strength and then you can do the wiring. If you are planning to repot a tree, then the wiring needs to have been carried out before the repotting, so that you can then leave the tree alone to recover. The last thing you want to be doing is pulling a recently repotted tree all over the place with an application of wire.

With deciduous trees, the best time to wire is in spring just before the buds open. The sap is starting to flow, so the branches are a little bit more flexible and forgiving, but they are still bare, so you don't have to deal with interfering foliage, which is easily damaged. Evergreen shrubs could also be wired at this time before delicate buds start to emerge.

Pines are best wired between September and April. Once the candles start to extend, they are fragile and easily damaged. The new spring growth on other conifers such as *Taxus*, spruce and cedar is also delicate, so they are often best left until autumn when the new growth has matured. I have generally wired junipers at all times of year and, provided the tree is healthy, have not experienced any problems. Be wary of carrying out any serious bending of heavy branches or trunks in the depths of winter. When the sap is not flowing and the temperature drops, they are very prone to snapping with no warning and just a loud crack.

Most of the work we carry out on Satsuki azaleas, such as pruning, wiring and repotting, is generally done immediately after flowering. Larch we tend to wire over the winter after they have dropped all their needles.

If you have a tree that is producing a lot of back-budding inside, you have to consider whether to let the buds develop further, and then carry out the wiring; or perhaps it is easier to wire now, but take great care to ensure that your wire is placed around the buds without causing damage.

When you have completed the extensive wiring of a tree, it is best to give it a sheltered position for a while and maybe also consider some winter protection just to help it recover.

Removing the Wire

We want the wire to stay on the tree as long as possible, which is another reason why you should develop a neat wiring style. The longer the wire stays on, the more likely it is that the branches will be set in place. I have wired specimen conifer bonsai in copper and, apart from removing some of the heavier wires, I have been able to leave almost all the wire on for four years. It is a case of trying to develop a wiring style that looks neat, is functional but at the same time still leaves the branch with some room to grow.

After a while, when you are carrying out your routine maintenance tasks, you need to look over your wired trees to check if the wire is starting to bite in. The age of the tree and how vigorous it is will influence how quickly it outgrows the wire and when it needs to be removed. With conifers, we can get away with letting the wire bite in a little, as this will help set the branches in place. When the wire is removed, any marks will be hidden from view all year round because of the foliage, and as the bark extends around these marks, it will conceal them and often add ageing character to the branch.

We have already acknowledged that with deciduous trees the bark can swell much more quickly and the wire will soon bite in. The problem here is that once the tree loses its leaves, any wire scars will become clearly visible and can be very unsightly. It can also take a deciduous tree a very long time to grow out these scars. We try to get the wire on as soon as we can in spring because if it is a young tree growing strongly, we may have to remove it during the summer.

You may be able to carefully unravel some of the wire in full lengths to remove it, but you have to be careful not to damage foliage and buds. In some areas, and often with the heavier gauge wires, you have no option but to cut it off. Most copper wire will have to be cut off because it is now set solid and no longer pliable. You may be able to straighten some of the reasonable-sized aluminium wire for re-use on training material in the ground, but you are always better using new wire wherever possible. Once used, it loses some of its strength and will never sit comfortably when re-applied to new branches because some of the previous twists and turns are still inherent in its make-up.

From making that first start in the initial styling of your bonsai to carrying out refinement work on a top-quality specimen bonsai, wiring has an important part to play. Every time we wire a tree, we are taking it to its next level. It may seem like an onerous task to start with, but it can become very therapeutic. It is a task you will find very rewarding to master.

The wire on this pine tree has bitten in so badly that we may lose some branches in trying to remove it. Wire scars exposing the cambium layer under the bark will be treated with wound sealant.

Beginners improvise with general and electrical pliers for cutting wire, but when it comes to removing wire, the specialist bonsai wire-cutter comes into its own, as it cuts right at the tip.

CHAPTER 4

INDOOR BONSAI

Introduction

I very briefly described what is meant by indoor bonsai towards the end of Chapter 1. So, to recap, most of the trees sold as indoor bonsai in the West are imported from China. You may also come across some Mediterranean varieties sold as indoor bonsai, such as olives and pomegranate. In their natural environment, the indoor bonsai are sub-tropical or tropical species that grow naturally as large trees or shrubs outside. When you keep this tree inside your home, you are basically trying to recreate its natural environment artificially. If you live in a more tropical climate, then you would be able to grow these species as outdoor bonsai.

For many people, receiving an indoor tree as a gift is their first introduction to the world of bonsai. Unfortunately, too many people end up losing their tree through being given bad advice or no help whatsoever. If you intend buying yourself an indoor bonsai, be sure to check out the advice at the beginning of Chapter 2 under sources of bonsai material, which outlines things to look out for and potential problems to avoid. Hopefully this current chapter will guide you through the practicalities of looking after your tree, keeping it alive and developing it further.

Right: A typical broom-style imported Chinese elm bonsai.

Ligustrum or Chinese privet with a slightly brighter, more delicate leaf than our common privet.

This tall *Ficus* has been trained in the literati-style.

Common Varieties

Chinese Elm (*Ulmus parvifolia*)

This is the most common variety of indoor tree that you are likely to encounter. It is imported and sold in large numbers, largely because of its resilience and durability. These factors make it ideal for people starting out with their first bonsai, where a greater tolerance is required whilst they master the basics. If it is allowed to dry out or if it gets too wet, it will drop all its leaves to take pressure off the roots and then happily re-bud if favourable conditions are restored and maintained. It has natural-looking bark, small leaves and easily develops fine twigs, so it really does look like a miniature tree, even in the smaller sizes.

I used to keep my Chinese elm with my outdoor bonsai and let it lose its leaves and go totally dormant in the winter. Just be wary though, it has a soft, sappy root system and will only stand temperatures down to about −3°C. The other thing you need to appreciate is that it is allergic to systemic sprays, so if you do get a bug infestation, just use a contact spray.

I would recommend this species of tree to anyone looking to purchase their first bonsai.

Ligustrum (Chinese Privet)

This tree is very similar in appearance to the common hedging privet that we often come across still surrounding many front gardens. The leaves do tend to be a little brighter in appearance and perhaps are not as robust. Just like its hedging cousin, it does respond well to pruning, throwing out many finer, new shoots.

Ficus

The varieties you are likely to encounter include *Ficus retusa* and, with a smaller leaf, *Ficus benjamina*. These trees really enjoy a humid atmosphere, so you may find it suitable for a kitchen or bathroom environment, provided it can be given adequate light. When branches are pruned, the tree will exude a white sap but don't be alarmed – it is sealing the cut and will soon stop.

Sagaretia theezans

Compared with *Ligustrum*, the *Sagaretia* leaf is similarly oval but paler, slightly smaller and much more delicate. As the tree ages, the grey outer layer of bark begins to peel away

An informal *Sagaretia* sending out new growth after a recent pruning.

Serissa can really struggle if the compost becomes waterlogged. Notice the brown/yellow tips at the end of the few remaining leaves.

to reveal a speckled, rich-brown trunk below. This process can create a dramatic appearance with a sense of greater age. Flowers are inconspicuous but it is capable of producing small, black, round berries.

Serissa foetida

This tree is affectionately known as 'the tree of a thousand stars' because of the large number of tiny star-shaped flowers it is capable of displaying. The leaves are also tiny and glossy. If you want flowers then you have to let new shoots extend and the tree will become a little untidy. Prune back to shape after flowering or if lengthened shoots are not showing any flower buds. If you meticulously keep it pruned to shape, it is unlikely to flower because it flowers on the tips of the new current season's growth. There is also a variegated form that can produce purple flowers. Its roots and shoots can give off a pungent smell when cut.

Ilex crenata (Japanese Holly)

This variety is imported from China cultivated as an indoor bonsai, trained and planted in traditional small bonsai pots. It is the same species that is cultivated in Japan to create the large ornate cloud trees, which are generally associated with Japanese gardens. Don't assume that because of this it can be kept outdoors during the winter. The Chinese tree is tender and should be kept frost-free over the winter months. Once again, it is a variety that responds well to pruning.

Carmona (Fukien Tea Tree)

There are two varieties you are likely to come across; *macrophylla* and, with a slightly smaller leaf size, *microphylla*. Both varieties can produce flowers and red berries but the flowers are so small as to be almost insignificant. These trees tend to be more tropical in their demands and many customers have

An informal upright *Ilex* that has been recently repotted.

struggled to keep them alive, especially if they have allowed the rootball to dry out. As a result of this, many importers stopped dealing in *Carmona*. However, I still have several clients who have had *Carmona* bonsai for many years and continue to take advantage of my repotting service.

Chinese Pepper Tree (*Xanthoxylum piperitum*)

This tree has dark-green, glossy leaves, which are long, spindly and in style reminiscent of some of our mountain ash trees. It can produce small, yellow flowers and tiny, black, round berries. The trunk is capable of developing thorns too. Because of the spindly nature of the leaves, it is not as easy to shape the canopy into neat foliage clouds.

Position

Whenever I have come across a care sheet handed out with a purchased indoor bonsai, one of the most prominent early pieces of advice is something like 'avoid direct sunlight'. On reading this, the bonsai novice automatically assumes that

Carmona macrophylla in the process of being repotted.

A small pepper tree showing how each leaf actually has almost ten tiny side-leaves.

Basic Tools/Equipment

If you are just starting out with your first bonsai, you don't have to invest heavily in specialist tools. In these early days any tools you do need to provide assistance can simply be obtained by improvisation. An old pair of kitchen scissors could be used for pruning twigs and small branches. If, for any reason, you did have to remove something a bit larger, then you could resort to some garden secateurs. Make-up tweezers will help remove small, unwanted leaves, whilst an old fork could substitute for a rake when repotting. Pliers from the household toolkit can be used for helping to create deadwood and cutting/bending wire.

If you think your interest might just peak in one or two trees and a bit of dabbling, you could buy a cheap Chinese bonsai scissor, which will do the job fine and enable you to at least look the part. However, if your interest is gaining momentum (and trust me it will), save your money and invest in better-quality Chinese and Japanese bonsai tools. Invest in the right tool, look after it and you will only have to buy it once. Bonsai is a bit like DIY in this respect: if you have the right tools for the job, the task is so much easier and infinitely much more pleasurable.

I will look at the wide array of tools available in more detail in Chapter 5 because, once you start showing an interest in outdoor bonsai, suddenly things become much more serious.

My *Sagaretia* sits happily on a coffee table in a wide bay window.

the best place for the tree must be somewhere in the middle of the room. In the old days this usually meant on top of the 'telly' or on the mantelpiece. With this advice we are already on the downhill slope. The tree is a living plant, which, in its normal natural environment, grows outside; it needs light, as much as possible, so the best place is in, or as near to, a window as possible. I think the care sheet was trying to warn that direct sunlight can cause the tree to dry out. You just have to appreciate that the more sun coming through the window, then the quicker the tree will dry and the more frequently you will have to water it; but it really is important that the tree gets this light.

Bonsai are similar to other houseplants in that they may grow better in some rooms or windows than others, so you may have to experiment. *Serissa*, for example, prefers an east- or west-facing window. The bougainvillea pictured at the opening of this chapter really does brighten up my bathroom and my day. First of all, put the tree where you would like it to be, your preferred location, and see how it goes. If it thrives, then everyone is happy, job done. If it doesn't seem happy, maybe loses some vigour or colour, then try it in another room and see if it improves. Each time you water the tree, when you replace it in the window, turn it around so that it will grow evenly on both sides. If you leave it the same way all the time, the branches will grow towards the light causing disturbing growth patterns and the tree will look unbalanced.

When you first introduce the tree to your home or move it from an established position to somewhere new, there may be a period of initial shock. Just like us they don't like change, so it may just take a short while to adapt to its new surroundings. This initial shock could result in some leaves, usually older inner ones, just falling or changing colour and then dropping. Just keep your eye on the tree and carefully control the watering, as explained in the next section.

If the tree is in a window and you close the curtains at night, it would be ideal if you could move the tree into the room overnight, especially during the winter months. This would avoid it being trapped in a cold void between the window and the curtains. In the summer months the tree would enjoy being outside, but make sure you avoid any early or late frosts. The transition must be gradual, so avoid massive temperature differences when moving it in or out. If you move it outside on a red-hot day in full sun, the tender leaves will simply get scorched; so try and pick a cloudy day with moderate temperatures. Bring it back in overnight and after a few days you can then pick a mild night to leave it outside for good; you are gradually hardening it off for its new environment. As we leave summer and move towards autumn, as soon as the temperatures drop, bring it back inside.

Watering

People are often surprised when you tell them that not only is watering the most crucial element in looking after bonsai, but it is also the most difficult task to master. It's true, any idiot is capable of throwing some water over a plant, but getting the amount and the timing right is another matter. The intimate relationship between the tree's roots, the compost in the pot and the amount of water will ultimately lead you down the path to success or failure.

What you are trying to achieve is to give the tree a good soaking and then leave it until that moment when the tree has used all the water from the soil, and just as the compost dries, you give it a good soaking again. Until you get used to your tree, it is not a question of watering it every day or every other day, but a case of checking it each day until you reach that point when it needs watering again. You have to learn to let your tree and its compost tell you when it requires watering. If the leaves or shoots start to droop, you know it needs watering – this is a cry for help. You will find that as you become more familiar with your tree and its location, you will get into a routine and have a good idea when water will be required. If you have not watered the tree for a few days but have been checking it regularly and you get to the point where it's 'do I' or 'don't I', I would always say, if in doubt, water it.

The reason you need to learn to follow the tree is that during the year its water requirements will change. For example, on long, warm, summer days the tree will be using more water than in the shorter miserable days of winter, even though it may be kept totally inside. Similarly, if the tree is extending shoots and growing strongly in late spring/early summer, it will require more water than those times when it is perhaps just ticking over and not putting out much new growth.

The orientation of the window that the tree sits in may also have a bearing on its water requirements. A tree in a south-facing window may take up more water than a tree in a north-facing window, especially on hot summer days. Two trees sitting next to each other in the same window may have different water requirements. Different species, the size of the pot, the type of compost can all influence how much water the tree needs on a daily basis.

I am not trying to frighten you or make it sound really complicated. I am trying to get you to just think about what you are doing. It is fairly straightforward, the answer is in the tree or its pot, you just have to look and don't fall into the once or twice a week trap. In almost every case when beginners have problems with indoor bonsai or the tree dies, it is because it either dried out completely or the compost was too wet. Often problems emerge when you go on holiday and trust a neighbour or relative to take over the watering duties. I once made a national newspaper when it was discovered that I offered a tree-sitting service whilst people went on holiday. Unbelievable!

When it comes to actually giving the water, you can place the tree in a sink and use a watering can with a fine hose or a small jug. Just be careful and slow, you don't want to wash all the compost out of the pot with a sudden jet flow. Sometimes with imported trees the compost can become very hard and compacted so that when you water, most of it just runs off the surface and does not penetrate the depth of the pot. If this happens, run some water in the sink and submerge the whole pot for about five minutes. When you have finished watering, let the tree drain off and then you can put it back in its display position. Ceramic and plastic drip trays can be purchased to fit under the pot and catch any water that might escape once it is back on display. If you get the soil watering right, there is no need to worry about misting or wetting the foliage. This in itself can, in fact, lead to other problems.

Feeding

Giving your tree some nourishment will help to keep it strong and healthy. It will encourage new, prolonged growth, which will help you to develop and improve your tree. It will also help it recover from any pest/disease attack or stress brought about by things like under- or over-watering. A healthy tree is a happy tree.

There are various proprietary food products developed specifically for bonsai available from specialist nurseries and some garden centres. Some are in a liquid format, whilst others are in the form of crystals or granules. Always follow the manufacturer's instructions. They will usually recommend feeding from around February to October, which is basically the main growing period in the UK.

Just remember that if you don't feed your tree, it will not be as strong and healthy, but if other conditions are right, there is a good chance it will tick over and survive. If you over-feed your tree, you could kill it. So if you are busy and miss some scheduled feeds, when you are able to restart don't give it extra to try to catch up; just resume with the normal rate and pick up the old routine. When you have repotted a tree, leave it six weeks before you start feeding again, so that you are not likely to scorch any newly exposed fresh roots. If your tree is sick, stop feeding and don't resume until you see signs of new growth and health, which will indicate that the roots are functioning again. If you come home from work feeling sick, the last thing you want is to go out for a slap-up meal.

With this popular bonsai food, the yellow top also acts as a measuring cup.

Problems, Pests and Diseases

As you have probably already gathered, the main problems tend to be self-inflicted: either under- or over-watering. If leaves are dropping or going yellow/brown, especially at the tips, and the soil is really wet, don't water again until the soil is almost dry. Then try and get back into a correct routine. If you have let the tree dry out, then the leaves will become brittle and dry. We have already stated that one of the attributes of the Chinese elm is that it will drop its leaves to try to take pressure off the roots if it becomes too dry. The problem is that when something like this happens, people become determined to make sure that it doesn't happen again, so they start to give it plenty of water. If most of its leaves have died or dropped, it doesn't need a lot of water at this point because it is not functioning properly, so now we have the opposite problem – the tree becomes too wet. You have to follow the tree again. If it has dried out, then water it, remove the dead or damaged leaves, but don't water it again until the soil virtually dries out. Continue to monitor it and water it this way and you will find that, as it comes back and starts to recover, it will gradually start taking up more water and need watering more frequently.

The main pest problem that you are likely to encounter with indoor bonsai is aphids. Sometimes you will see them: greenfly, whitefly or blackfly. Sometimes their presence may be indicated by leaf discoloration and/or a residual stickiness. Follow the manufacturer's instructions and spray the tree with a proprietary systemic insecticide,

The heavy moss growth contributes to the wet compost, which has resulted in this Chinese elm dropping so many leaves.

The sticky residue of an aphid attack is clearly visible and often found on leaves inside or under the canopy.

repeating the treatment at the recommended intervals. Just remember that Chinese elms are allergic to systemic sprays so, in this instance, you will need to use a contact spray such as a 'bug gun'.

Avoid mist spraying or wetting the foliage, especially late at night, as this can lead to problems from mildew.

Repotting

When you acquire a new indoor bonsai it is unlikely that you will know when it was last repotted, unless you are purchasing from a bonsai nursery and they can confirm that the tree has been repotted since it was imported. The ideal time to repot is just as the tree is showing signs of new growth. With indoor bonsai this can vary but is often in the spring months when the tree has been just ticking over in winter due to the shorter hours of daylight. If the tree continues to grow strongly after the repotting, it will

April 2020 – a typical informal Chinese elm. As soon as you see new buds opening, it is a good time to repot.

help it recover more quickly from the stress of the repotting operation.

When you think the time is right, gently ease the tree out of the pot (there may be some tie wires to cut underneath) and examine the rootball. If the tree is not pot-bound, the compost is still open and there is ample room for the roots to develop further, you can drop the tree back in the pot and make a note to check it again the following year. If the roots are solid or severely coiled around the pot, then you will need to repot it. For a more detailed explanation and step-by-step guidance on how to do this, please refer to Chapter 6.

Once the tree has been repotted and watered, it can be returned to its normal position. Don't forget to not feed now for six weeks. We try to leave the tree as long as we can between each repotting, aiming for around four years. If the tree is growing well with no problems, then maybe after three years lift it out as before just to check the condition of the rootball. If everything is fine, then return it to the pot and just check it each following year until eventually the time comes when it will need repotting again.

Basic Pruning/Training

If you are content just looking after your one tree, then maybe all you want to do is keep it under control, especially if you are happy with its basic shape. Let new shoots elongate with about six new leaves and then simply prune back to the original profile of the tree. The elongation is essential because new shoots means new roots and you are building up the energy and strength of the tree. If you don't let the tree extend and you keep it continually held back, you are not letting it grow and it will gradually become weaker.

Within the overall canopy of the tree you are trying to create clouds of foliage and some spaces to allow light and air in. You can greatly improve the shape of your tree over a period of time just by using a 'clip and grow' topiary method. Just prune the extended shoots back with a little bit more thought with regard to their length, aiming to improve the tree's outline and the foliage clouds. There is a subtle difference in the way foliage clouds can be merged naturally and almost seamlessly together, rather than becoming distinct separate 'pom-poms' of foliage at the ends of branches.

As your interest, confidence and enthusiasm grows, there is no reason why you can't consider using some of the other techniques detailed in this book to take your little indoor bonsai to another level.

What Happens If You Don't Prune Your Bonsai?

When someone receives a bonsai as a gift, or maybe it is your very first tree, it is immediately precious and something that is cherished. Consequently, there is a reluctance to do anything to the tree that may cause it harm. Naturally, attacking it with a pair of scissors is way high up on the list of places not to go! The thought of damaging the tree, or getting it wrong, is simply overwhelming.

The problem is that if the tree is allowed to grow unchecked with no attempt made to restrain its extending growth, the vigour will just grow out of the tree. The tree will struggle to support all this foliage, which is now so far away from the trunk and roots. A few leaves at the ends of the growing tips will be kept but inner shoots and foliage will be sacrificed. The tree will completely lose its shape and its health will be jeopardized.

I hope the advice in this chapter of the book will inspire you and give you the confidence to prune your bonsai. Just remember, if the tree is healthy and growing well, if your pruning turns out not exactly as you intended, it will simply grow back and produce new shoots. Start from the outside and cut a bit at a time until you reach the length you want. You can cut more off; you can't stick bits back on!

Top Right: You can see how long the branches of this Chinese elm have been allowed to grow unchecked and the weakening effect on the inner branches.

Right: All is not lost. You simply have to prune back to the basic structure/shape and the tree will regrow its side branches and twigs.

Some Examples

May 2020 – the tree has been allowed to extend and has grown well in less than two months.

Top: Strong, upright growth is cut back. Above: Long side-shoots are cut back allowing a little extension to build up the profile of the tree.

The tree after pruning with some shorter new shoots left to extend further before being pruned back.

A group of three Chinese elms ready for pruning and we need to see more of the lower trunks to emphasize that sense of a natural landscape.

Now we have the basis for clouds of foliage but also spaces that make the tree look taller, whilst allowing light and air to penetrate the canopy.

A larger Chinese elm with a good, mature, triangular canopy, which has been allowed to extend and become a little untidy.

After pruning we still have the same overall canopy, but within this canopy we have clouds of foliage and spaces becoming more clearly defined.

Above: A large overgrown *Ficus* that may have started life as a houseplant.

Left: Drastic pruning required to prepare it for wiring and styling as a bonsai.

A sweet little Chinese elm with the lower branches wired outwards and allowed to extend because we need them to be thicker.

The branches pruned back and our basic structure is so much better. Now we can work on the secondary branches and twigs.

Case Study: *Sagaretia theezans*

1999 – I have had this tree for around twenty-five years, so you can keep bonsai alive indoors for a long period of time. It was originally laid flat in a long green Chinese pot. The lower branch moving towards the left would become very important!

2001 – the slanting style and lifting it more upright in the pot did appear to suit it, but the emphasis of the tree was moving away from its main feature. Here it is enjoying some summer sunshine outside.

2001 – the main reason I had been attracted to the tree was the amazing trunk. It tells the story of a tree of considerable age with amazing character. The cracked and charred deadwood almost suggests that the tree may have survived a fire at some point.

2014 – the top section had certainly become weaker and the upper, straight section did not work so well with the impressive lower trunk. So here it is in October with the upper canopy removed.

February 2017 – the tree is repotted in to a smaller pot, also by Derek Aspinall. The tree has no heavy roots, so under the soil becomes like a construction site to try to support the substantial trunk and canopy above.

6

2017 – the tree after the repotting with the upper section of removed trunk reduced in height. The canopy has been lightened to take pressure off the roots. I think this angle will ultimately finish up being the new front of the tree.

7

7 May 2020 – the tree is sprouting really well and ready for another pruning to keep it under control and produce more fine twigs around the edges of the canopy.

8

This Masakuni tweezer has a cutting blade ideal for dealing with soft, new growth at the branch tips. We can now use the tree's energy and good health to further improve its fine ramification.

Right: 8 May 2020 – after the second pruning and once again the lower branches are left untouched. Allowing them to extend is making use of the tree's energy, to keep it strong but at the same time allowing us to strictly control the growth of any upper twigs.

9

10

11

Above: 31 May 2020 – after yet another pruning session. You can now clearly see just how far the lower branches have extended. Eventually I will prune these back to the canopy and start to build foliage clouds on them in keeping with the rest of the tree.

Left: 31 May 2020 – the tree seen from the other side. This tree is making good progress and it shows that not only can you enjoy some longevity with indoor bonsai, but they can also be a really worthwhile ongoing project.

CHAPTER 5

OUTDOOR BONSAI

Introduction

Outdoor trees are what almost every serious bonsai enthusiast is growing and developing. For the vast majority, indoor bonsai may be something that introduces them to the hobby or fires up an interest, but they are soon dropped in favour of the outdoor species. Basically, this group includes every tree that is not traditionally sold or grown as an indoor bonsai. In most cases, these trees are being grown in their natural or local climate, so they are already happier with their environment. It is easy to see why people are drawn to these trees. Many of us were initially fired up by pictures of classic specimen bonsai in Japan, such as pines, junipers and maples. The attraction of the many amazing flowering and fruiting varieties simply needs no explanation. Some people are inspired by indigenous full-size trees that they have encountered whilst out walking. There is a plentiful supply of outdoor shrub and plant material both in our gardens and nurseries that we can practise on and develop.

Please check out the advice at the beginning of Chapter 2 if you are thinking of purchasing an established bonsai from a specialist nursery. Before you can start developing and progressing your bonsai, you have to be able to keep them alive and healthy. This chapter will cover the practicalities of care and, hopefully, give you the confidence and knowledge to start you on the road to success.

Common Varieties

Pines

The pine bonsai, which originated in Japan, that you are likely to encounter, are the white pine (*Pinus pentaphylla* on its own roots or *Pinus parviflora* grafted on to black pine rootstock), the black pine (*Pinus thunbergii*) and the red pine (*Pinus densiflora*). The white pine is weaker on its own roots and generally more problematic to look after, as it does not like being kept too wet. You may also come across the grafted smaller needle varieties of white pine, *kokonoe* and *zuisho*. Most pines we use in bonsai are two-needle pines, but the white pine has five needles growing out of each sheath.

In Europe, the pines that you are most likely to find in the wild and in nurseries are the many varieties of Scots pine (*Pinus sylvestris*) and the mugo pine (*Pinus mugo*).

Junipers

The most popular varieties for bonsai are *Juniperus chinensis* and *Juniperus ittogawa*. These offer compact, dense foliage growth capable of being shaped into attractive foliage clouds. Any old yamadori trees imported from Japan you may encounter are likely to be *Juniperus sargentii*, a juniper native to Japan and with coarser

White pines pictured here in quarantine shortly after arriving from Japan.

Juniperus chinensis ittogawa imported from Japan in the spring and pictured here in July after being released from quarantine and potted on.

foliage. Another import from Japan is the needle juniper (*Juniper rigida*), which, as its name suggests, can be a prickly tree to deal with.

In Europe, you may come across the common juniper (*Juniperus communis*) collected from the wild, whilst some varieties of this species are also available in garden centres. *Juniperus sabina* is another popular yamadori juniper collected extensively in parts of Spain and Italy. Most of the juniper varieties you will find in garden centres make good raw material for bonsai and include *Procumbens, Pfitzeriana, Parsonii* and members of the *Squamata meyerii* family.

An old Ezo spruce originally imported from Japan.

Other Conifers

There are other conifers capable of producing excellent bonsai:

- You will encounter several varieties of spruce (*Picea abies*) in garden centres and may even come across yamadori trees collected from the mountains of Europe. There have also been some fine spruce imported from Japan in the past (*Picea jezoensis*) known as the Ezo spruce.
- The yew tree is popular with bonsai enthusiasts, whether it be *Taxus baccata* or the Japanese *Taxus cuspidata*.
- The hinoki cypress (*Chamaecyparis obtusa nana gracilis*) makes an attractive tree with its rich flaky bark and two-tone bright green foliage.
- *Cryptomeria*, the Japanese cedar, is seldom seen as bonsai in Europe but is popular in Japan.
- The larch is often referred to as a deciduous conifer because it loses its needles in winter. It is a popular bonsai species, whether it be as an individual tree or a forest planting. The European larch (*Larix decidua*) has straw-coloured new growth, whereas the Japanese larch (*Larix kaempferi*) has more orange-coloured new shoots.

Maples

There are literally hundreds of varieties of maple (*Acer palmatum*), with many being available in most garden centres, whilst larger selections can be found in specialist maple nurseries. The popular bonsai maples imported from Japan include the standard green or mountain maple, the dwarf, smaller-leaved Kiyohime and Kashima, together with the very popular spring red/pink-leaved Deshojo, Seigen, Benichidori and Chisio. You may also encounter Shishigashira, with very tight, crinkly, green-leaved foliage. The other popular imported bonsai subject is the trident maple (*Acer beurgerianum*), whose leaves have three lobes as opposed to the five normally associated with most acers.

Many of the maple varieties are grafted near the base on to a more vigorous commercial rootstock. Some of these grafts can be ugly and disrupt the flow of the trunk, which is not a problem for the gardener but for bonsai purposes a good, almost invisible graft is crucial. The popular imported bonsai varieties are tried and tested, respond well to our training techniques but, more importantly, will generally have an excellent graft.

By all means experiment with the many different varieties that you may come across in garden centres, but make sure that you start with a good graft, a tapering trunk and, if possible, a reasonable, existing branch structure. Some of the larger-leaved varieties may prove stubborn to reduce in size and the popular Dissectum and Atropurpureum

A Deshojo maple in late May with the red spring foliage just starting to turn green for the summer.

A *Ginkgo biloba* starting to show its autumn glory. The natural canopy form of this tree is often likened to the flame of a candle.

varieties do not produce a second flush of growth as readily as the imported bonsai maples. Some of these garden varieties are still capable of producing excellent bonsai, it may just take you a bit longer to achieve the desired result.

Other Deciduous Trees

Many people come in to bonsai as a result of collecting self-sown seedlings that they have found in their garden or whilst out walking, so most indigenous species are naturally popular bonsai subjects. The ones I encounter regularly in classes include:

- Oak (*Quercus robur*)
- Hawthorn (*Crataegus*)
- Hornbeam (*Carpinus betulus*)
- Beech (*Fagus sylvatica*)
- Common field maple (*Acer campestre*)
- Elm (*Ulmus procera*)
- Gingko (*Gingko biloba*)
- Lime tree (*Tilia cordata*)

Beginners will often try with sycamore (*Acer pseudoplatanus*), chestnut (*Aesculus*) and ash (*Fraxinus* or *Sorbus*), but it can take years of correct and careful cultivation to get the leaf size down to a manageable scale.

Other popular imported bonsai deciduous trees you may come across include the Korean hornbeam (*Carpinus coreana*), Japanese white beech (*Fagus crenata*), Japanese elm (*Zelkova serrata*) and stewertia (*Stewertia monodelpha*).

We already know that tried and tested species can produce excellent results as bonsai in a relatively short period of time, so starting with these can make life easier. But be prepared to have a go with anything that comes your way, especially if it is free. It all helps with the learning process and you may be pleasantly surprised with the results of your efforts.

Flowering and Fruiting Trees and Shrubs

As stated in the brief introduction, the appeal of this group of trees is fairly obvious. For a brief period during the seasons these trees will become the star of your display, capable of lifting your spirits and capturing the heart of anyone who visits your garden. Most trees and shrubs that you cultivate as garden plants have the potential for being trained as bonsai and are capable of producing amazing results. The smaller the leaf size, the easier it will be to produce a miniature tree that looks the part. Hedging material that responds well to being regularly pruned back makes excellent bonsai, so be sure to consider *Cotoneaster, Pyracantha, Ligustrum* (privet), *Lonicera* and *Berberis*.

You may also consider wisteria, flowering cherries (*Prunus mume* and *Prunus serrulata*), various crab apple varieties (*Malus*), quince (Japanese *Chaenomeles* or Chinese *Pseudocydonia sinensis*), winter jasmine (*Jasminum nudiflorum*), *Elaeagnus, Euonymus* and mulberry (*Morus*).

The stunning Satsuki azaleas (*Rhododendron indicum*), imported from Japan, offer hundreds of varieties, some producing different-coloured flowers on the same tree. Flowering species imported from Japan as bonsai are often more reliable at producing flowers, both immediately and regularly. If you are buying raw material from a garden centre, it is good if you can see it in flower because then you can see exactly what you are buying, but, more importantly, you know it is capable of producing flowers. Wisteria, for example, generally has to be at least seven years old before it starts flowering.

The contrast between the emerging fresh new growth and the well-distributed, delicate pink flowers on this Satsuki azalea is simply delightful.

Not content with just white spring flowers, this *Cotoneaster* is determined to be an autumn/winter star with an amazing show of red berries.

Tools/Equipment

As a beginner it can be quite daunting if you visit a bonsai nursery and see the vast array of tools available. You don't have to invest in these tools all at once and, as outlined in Chapter 4, you can improvise with household items to get you started. Specific tools have been developed over the years to make it easier for you to carry out all the styling, pruning and repotting work on your bonsai. Larger tools may be required if you are working on a substantial piece of raw material, whilst smaller tools may be more appropriate for refinement work on an established bonsai; so many of the tools are available in different sizes. Some people prefer the stainless finished tools, which tend to be a little more expensive, but the black carbon-finished tools are also adequate for the tasks in hand. In addition to the Japanese tools, there are now good-quality Chinese tools available and both will serve you well. If you are serious about the hobby, don't buy cheap tools; it really is false economy. When I started out, Christmas and birthdays were a great way of enlarging my toolkit. With the less used tools, you can acquire these once you have a specific task to complete.

It really is important to have at least one good pair of scissors. The two on the left are used more for twig pruning, whilst the two on the right are a more general purpose scissor. I use the one on the right for all my root work and use a separate scissor for pruning branches.

The first serious tool you need to acquire is a branch/concave cutter. This enables you to cut branches off flush with the trunk, whereas improvising with secateurs will leave a snag. The two on the left are the normal concave cutter, whilst the right one is a round blade, concave cutter, which can also be used like a knob cutter.

The left tool is a root pruner also used for carving deadwood. The middle tool is a trunk splitter used for splitting and tearing deadwood. The right tool is a knob cutter that enables you to prune a branch off at the trunk, leaving a small hollow, which helps the wound to callous over and heal more naturally.

The tool on the left is a wire-cutter. There are other styles but all do the same job. The other tools are both jin pliers used for stripping and tearing bark to create deadwood. The straight jin plier is also used for twisting the wire when tying a tree into the pot after repotting.

The rakes are used to untangle and comb out the roots when repotting, whilst the tweezers pick out dead leaves/pluck needles from the canopy. The chopsticks can help to untangle the roots and also to work the new compost into the roots to complete the repotting. The spatula is used to smooth down the soil and loosen tight edges.

Examples of carving tools for creating deadwood. The knife is also used for grafting and layering work. Nylon, steel and brass brushes are available for cleaning the bark and deadwood. The nylon brush is softer for more delicate work, whilst the other brushes are ideal in more aggressive situations.

The black mesh is cut into small pieces to cover the drainage holes. The plastic and stainless sets of three scoops are used for distributing the new compost in to the pot when repotting. You will notice the larger stainless scoop incorporates a mesh for sieving out any fine dust in the compost.

Interchangeable mesh sieves with three inserts, each having different-sized holes. This is invaluable when mixing bonsai composts, as it enables you to remove any fine dust, which would clog up the drainage holes. It also allows you to mix composts of different particle size for different-sized pots but also for different positions in the same pot.

Position

Your bonsai should be positioned outside so that it can take full advantage of its natural environment and the changing seasons. It's even better if you can create a display setting near to your house so that the tree is happy outside but you can still enjoy its presence from a window or patio door. A light, open, airy location with the tree receiving sun for at least part of the day is ideal. Some trees, like yew and the maples, will tolerate dappled shade, but trees are unlikely to thrive in a dark, shaded corner with minimal airflow and starved of light. If the foliage on your tree takes on a particularly dark hue, this could indicate that it is not getting enough sun. Most trees will tolerate full sun provided you can keep on top of their water requirements. If you are at home most of the day to check the compost, this can be fine. However, if you are leaving the tree all day in full sun, in the middle of a hot summer, then you need to make sure it is well watered before you leave home. The tree will be even more susceptible if it stands alone on an elevated pillar fully exposed to all weather conditions.

Pictures of specimen bonsai in Japan standing shoulder to shoulder on long benches always look impressive, but the trees are also giving each other some protection from the elements. Turning your trees at regular intervals will ensure a more even distribution of the weather over the foliage, leading to normal natural growth patterns. This becomes particularly important if your display bench is next to a wall or fence, as all branches will grow towards the light and not naturally outwards.

Winter in the bonsai garden does come with a certain charm but also presents the enthusiast with a whole new set of challenges.

The amount of protection required for your trees in winter will depend on the severity of the winters in your location. Recent winters in the UK have been fairly mild and trees have been happy outside in their normal setting with limited protection. A cold greenhouse is ideal to over-winter your trees; just make sure it is well ventilated and don't forget to check the compost regularly, so that you know when to water. If your trees have to remain outside, then keep a watchful eye on the extreme weather fore-casts. If forecasters are expecting extreme cold, freezing temperatures, persistent heavy rain or snow, severe gales or freezing winds, this is when your trees will require addi-tional protection. You could bring the trees into a cold shed or garage and then put them back out as soon as the extremes have passed. Don't suddenly bring them inside your warm centrally heated home; this could start to break their winter dormancy too early.

Some enthusiasts put their trees under the benches and then drape some heavy-duty polythene over the benches to enclose the trees when the weather turns bad. Placing your trees on the ground is not such a bad thing in this scenario, as the temperature there will not be as cold as on the elevated bench and they will not be as exposed to cold, prevailing winds. Wrapping the pots in bubble wrap can provide another layer of protection when adverse conditions persist.

Frozen Bonsai

It is important that your trees are exposed to the first early frosts of autumn, as this will trigger the trees' natural hardening processes against the cold winter weather to come. Trees can, to varying degrees, withstand the freezing of the soil in the pot (it is actually the water in the soil that freezes) but most problems seem to arise if the above-ground temperature suddenly rises or if the foliage is exposed to cold, drying winds. Water is lost from the foliage and branches, and cannot be adequately replaced from the still-frozen roots. This can result in branches or the tree itself dying over the winter period. So, cold wind protection externally and avoiding high temperature rises in greenhouses can be critical issues. This is why trees can be more vulnerable when we have nights that are very cold with freezing temperatures followed by days of full winter sun and clear, blue skies. Susceptibility to these freezing winter conditions varies between species with Chinese elm and trident maple being particularly vulnerable.

Avoid having your bonsai area exposed to strong, pre-vailing winds. The tender leaves of maples will blacken and shrivel in such a location. Beware of tunnelling effects in your garden; for example, if wind is channelled down a side passage that is in line with your bonsai display, you may notice that this impacts on growth and condition on trees directly exposed.

Watering

I make no apologies for repeating some of the advice I gave on watering in Chapter 4, it really is so important to get it right. In many cases it is the difference between success and failure.

As I said before, what you are trying to achieve is to give the tree a good soaking and then leave it until that moment when the tree has used all the water from the soil and, just as the compost dries, you give it a good soaking again. Initially you may have to check your tree every day to determine when it needs watering, but you will soon get used to its requirements. Drooping leaves or shoots means you have probably let it go too long with-out water. If ever you are in doubt as to whether to water or not, I would always say water it. You will soon get into your own routine.

You have to learn to follow and understand your trees. Different compost types, different pot sizes, different health conditions and different times of year will all influ-ence how often a tree needs water. Phew! And you haven't turned the tap on yet! For example, on long, warm summer days in the heart of the growing season, trees will be using more water than in the shorter miserable days of winter when they are dormant or just ticking over. Trees will require more water at times when they are covered in flowers or carrying a heavy crop of fruit. Trees in very small or shallow pots will need more scrutiny than perhaps those in large, deep pots. Deciduous trees in full leaf will gener-ally take up more water than conifers. The weather conditions and how free-draining your compost is will affect how often you water. Trees you have acquired from different sources are likely to be in different compost mixes, just to complicate matters further. If a tree has been recently repotted or sick, its roots may not be fully func-tional and, therefore, its water requirements are likely to be less than your adjacent healthy trees.

I apologize once again for frightening you but I am trying to make you realize that watering is not about turning on some automatic sprinkler while you slope off somewhere else. You really do need to think about what you are doing, assess the task in hand and carry it out accordingly. Get this right and your trees will show their appreciation with vibrant foliage colour and strong healthy growth.

If you have just a few trees, then you can use a watering can fitted with a fine rose. As (or rather when) your collection expands, you may find it easier to use a hosepipe with a fine-spray attachment. It's a case of being able to thoroughly wet the soil, allowing the water to penetrate and filter through, without washing the compost out of the pot. Make sure you water all of the pot and don't create a perennial dry spot behind the trunk. Some people prefer to water in the evening, whilst others prefer the morning. Ultimately, I think it is how best the timing fits in with your lifestyle and daily routine. If you do water in the evening, try to make sure you are allowing sufficient time for any wet foliage to dry out, as this can lead to overnight fungal problems as the temperature drops. Watering the foliage of deciduous trees in full sun can lead to problems from scorching, especially if you have not wet the compost first.

I watered my own private collection using these two Japanese copper watering cans and the covered water basin on which they sit.

Feeding

There is no substitute for the two main ingredients for plant growth: namely, sun and water. Hopefully, if you have taken on board the previous section, you now have some control over the water, whilst I do concede that the amount of sun your trees get will, to a large degree, be out of your hands. Feeding, then, is more akin to a supplement to try and bolster up the main ingredients.

All the points raised in Chapter 4 about feeding indoor bonsai, also relate to the feeding of outdoor trees. So remember not to over-feed your trees, allow around six weeks after repotting before you recommence feeding and don't feed sick trees until they are showing strong signs of recovery.

In my early bonsai years I used traditional chemical plant foods from the local garden centre, basically because this was all I had access to. Now, you will find that there are numerous products specifically formulated for feeding bonsai available from the specialist nurseries or online. Always follow the manufacturer's instructions with regard to the amount of food given and the frequency of the applications. For many years now my feeding regime has been based on a monthly application of a slow-release, balanced, granular fertilizer. Nitrogen will be fairly quickly washed out of the soil with intense watering, so it is important that we replenish it on a regular basis. Feeding on the

I currently use Naruko from Japan. Larger food pellets are placed under baskets anchored to the soil.

first day of every month is an easy routine to adopt and to remember. I would supplement this around the middle of the month with a liquid-based, foliar feed.

Problems, Pests and Diseases

Keeping your tree strong and healthy will help it to avoid attracting problems in the first place and, if it does succumb to a pest or disease, it will be in a much better position to fight it off and survive. Bonsai trees are prone to all the normal pests and diseases that you are likely to encounter both in your garden and in the wild. Unlike garden and wild plants, they have a diligent servant keeping a regular watchful eye over their general wellbeing, which should ensure that any problems are detected quickly and dealt with before they can pose a serious threat.

Aphids

Greenfly, blackfly and whitefly are more prevalent during the spring and the summer months. Sometimes in spring, fresh young shoots take on the guise of thick, black stems engulfed in blackfly. They often occur on hidden low and internal branches, especially under a dense canopy, making them harder to spot until the infestation is well established. Maples seem to be particularly vulnerable. They often leave behind a sticky honeydew excretion on leaves and needles, which sometimes can also take on a black sooty appearance, especially in damp conditions. It is often this stickiness on the upper surface of leaves that actually alerts you to the attack in the first place. White, fluffy, woolly aphids can often form dense groups on the underside of beech leaves. Woolly aphid-like infestations can also be found on pines and larch.

Many invading pests don't want to kill their host, after all it is helping them to survive and thrive. However, a severe attack can seriously weaken your tree and inhibit new growth, especially as it often comes early in the growing season. In this instance, a tree may just limp along for the whole growing year just trying to survive.

Once you identify the problem, you need a proprietary systemic insecticide spray from your local garden centre. Always follow the manufacturer's instructions and make

An army of blackfly rampant on a fresh young shoot with the sticky residue clearly visible on the adjoining leaves.

sure that you also spray underneath the leaves and inside the tree's canopy. Repeat the spraying at intervals recommended by the manufacturer until you feel confident the infestation has been dealt with.

Caterpillars

Damaged, partly eaten, unsightly leaves are often an indication that you have resident caterpillars. In most cases the damage is only slight and does not seriously harm the tree, but it can have an impact on appearance, especially if you are planning to exhibit your tree. A severe attack can cause some weakening of the tree and affect seasonal growth, just like the aphid infestation.

This caterpillar has perfected the art of disguise and it's quite a shock when the small branch you are about to prune suddenly moves.

You can just make out the small, yellow larvae in this 'cuckoo spit', that feed on sap and can be removed by hand.

Particularly on *Pyracantha* and azaleas, a protective film down the centre of the leaf, which often folds, will be home to small sawfly larvae.

A cluster of scale insect on a deciduous tree clearly showing their protective shells.

A fairly heavy infestation of white scale insects on a juniper bonsai with early signs of some dieback.

Scale Insects

Their protective shell is often visible on the stems and leaves of trees. They are a sap-feeding insect often accompanied by the honeydew extract and sooty mould associated with aphids and described earlier. I have generally found that removal by hand is the best way to deal with this problem.

Juniper scale is identified by small, white shapes laid on the foliage and can often be accompanied by the honeydew stickiness as well. A shaking of the tree will often see small white dust-like particles falling to the ground. Badly affected shoots will go yellow and brown before dying back. Sometimes it just sucks the colour out of the tree, leaving the foliage a miserable grey rather than vibrant green. It can take as long as two seasons for the colour to return and requires the regular spraying of an appropriate systemic insecticide.

Vine Weevil

This small, black beetle that you may come across in summer does not really do a lot of damage herself other than maybe chew on a few leaves. Her biggest threat is that she will lay eggs in your pots. These eggs will hatch as small, white grubs with a brown tip that simply love to feed on your tree's roots. She can't fly, so any pots you have on the ground are the most vulnerable. She prefers a soft, soil-based compost rather than those that are almost entirely granular. I only tend to find the grubs in akadama when the medium has almost completely broken down and the tree is ready for repotting.

This small black beetle may only be about 1cm in length but the grubs from the eggs she lays can ravage a tree's root system.

Her strategy for laying the eggs is a very haphazard affair. I once had a row of training material in plant pots and when we came to repot one found sixty-four grubs (still a record here) in the soil. I hastily repotted all the other trees fearing the worst and didn't find another single grub. The thing is not to panic if you find a beetle or grub. Make a note of the tree and other trees in close proximity, keep an eye on them and only intervene if you notice a problem or when you can check the roots at the correct time of year. I have known enthusiasts find a beetle, panic, repot their entire collection at the wrong time of year and do more damage than a rampant herd of beetles could have caused! Several proprietary treatments for this pest are available from most garden centres.

Fungal Problems

If you mist-spray your trees or wet the foliage when watering, make sure it has time to dry before nightfall. As the overnight temperatures drop, damp foliage is more prone to being affected by mildew, especially if they are in a shady location with little air movement. A grey powdery coating

This fungus affecting trident maples causes leaves to remain small with discoloration and dieback around the edges.

will form on the leaf surfaces and, in extreme cases, can affect other areas of the tree and cause dieback. Remove affected leaves and spray with an appropriate systemic fungicide, following the manufacturer's instructions.

Some deciduous trees, like hawthorn, can be affected by peach leaf curl, especially if there are fruit trees growing in your neighbourhood. A species of *Gymnosporangium* fungus can also affect fruit trees and junipers. You will find it as a bright yellow/orange soft fungus growth, which eventually turns to a scale-like growth on the bark and results in the girth of the trunk thickening at the point of outbreak.

Fortunately, the leaves on this Kiyohime maple had matured sufficiently so that the overnight frost damage was not too severe.

This seems particularly attracted to *Pfitzeriana* varieties but I have also encountered it on *Juniper procumbens* too. Remove the fungus tissue on discovery and spray with a systemic fungicide to try to inhibit the transmission cycle.

A rust-like fungus can affect trident maples, causing the leaves to remain very small and not develop fully, with brown discoloration around the edges. This can weaken specific areas of the tree or the whole tree if the problem is widespread. Spray the whole tree with a systemic fungicide on discovery and repeat the application in line with the manufacturer's instructions. I would also spray the tree every other month during the winter when it is dormant and again as the leaves are emerging. It may take several seasons to fully eradicate the problem.

The Weather

A mild spell in early spring can bring your trees to life with buds bursting and soft new growth emerging. Late, overnight frosts can cause severe damage to any tender, new growth. At this time of year you have to keep a lookout for warnings of extreme weather conditions, so that you can take steps to protect any vulnerable trees.

In the summer, with trees growing strongly and carrying a heavy canopy of leaves, it becomes especially important to make sure that they don't dry out, otherwise you could be faced with brown, shrivelled leaves on the exposed outer areas.

Hardening-Off

If you have protected your trees over winter, such as in a greenhouse or polytunnel, it is important that when you move them back outside, you do this as a gradual process. Don't suddenly move them from a cosy, mild, protected environment inside to a harsh, cold, exposed position outside. Try and pick a calm, mild day when you first place them back outside, and then bring them back inside overnight. Repeat this for a few days until you can pick a favourable mild night to then leave them out all the time. This phasing process will harden the tree, lessen the shock and help it to adapt to its return to the outside. When you start this process, avoid also any hot, full-sun days, as any new foliage will be tender and will easily burn. An overcast, cloudy day is ideal and these are generally plentiful in the UK! In spring I try to let my maples and other deciduous trees come into leaf outside.

Repotting

Most of the advice given in Chapter 4 on repotting indoor trees also applies to outdoor trees. When you acquire a new tree, try to find out when it was last repotted, otherwise it may be prudent to lift the tree out of the pot at the earliest correct opportunity to examine the rootball and determine yourself when it will need repotting. For most trees, the best time to repot is in spring when you see the buds starting to change colour or swell. You know then that the tree is ready to start growing and this will aid its recovery from the stressful repotting operation. New growth means that the tree will be producing new roots. In the UK, we normally start with larch, maples and other deciduous trees in February, followed by yews, pines, junipers and other conifers as we progress through March and into April. Satsuki azaleas are normally pruned and repotted after they have finished flowering, which is usually around July. We could repot other flowering trees, such as crab apples, after they have finished flowering, but the problem is that many of these trees start producing leaf growth before the flowers have finished and, therefore, the window of opportunity is very small. It is often safer and easier to repot these trees earlier, just as the flower buds start to move.

When you examine the rootball, you are looking for fine, brown, white-tipped, healthy roots and space in the compost for the roots to continue to grow. If the pot is full of roots and the compost has disappeared or the roots are just tightly encircling the pot, then you will have to repot the tree. If there is still looseness in the soil and space for further root growth, then you can drop the tree back in the pot for another year.

We want to leave the tree in the pot for as many years as we safely can. This will help refine the growth and age the appearance of the tree generally. The less frequently we have to subject the tree to this process, the better. I generally aim for about four or five years between repotting. For really old trees this gap will often be longer. Younger trees are generally more vigorous and will produce fresh new roots more quickly. Deciduous trees tend to produce a denser rootball more quickly than conifers. Obviously, strong, healthy trees will produce more roots than trees that are sick or struggling. These are some of the factors you will need to consider when deciding when your bonsai needs repotting.

For a more detailed explanation on the actual repotting process and step-by-step guidance, please refer to Chapter 6. Once your tree has been repotted, keep it in a calm, sheltered spot, giving it time to recover and don't start feeding for around six weeks.

Plenty of fine, healthy roots, but it's now a dense solid mass and the tree is ready for repotting.

Basic Pruning/Training

If you have a few outdoor trees and basically just want to keep them under control, then most of the basic pruning advice for indoor trees, detailed in Chapter 4, could equally be applied to your deciduous outdoor trees. You are trying to create a neat, triangular shape with some spaces between the branches. Occasionally, some thinning of inner foliage will be required to allow more light and air to enter the canopy, especially if it becomes a dense, solid mass.

Shoots growing downwards and emerging from below a branch are removed completely on both deciduous and coniferous trees. Upward-growing shoots are kept under control and pruned back to the profile of the narrow cloud of foliage that you are trying to create.

If your conifer bonsai has an established shape, it may be possible to exert some control by general pruning of branch extensions around the periphery of your tree.

Pines can be a bit more complicated and will be discussed in Chapter 8. In very basic terms, it may be easier for you to let them grow through the season and then around September (early Autumn) prune back any excessive, overly long growth. To be on the safe side, make sure

This Korean hornbeam has been allowed to grow unchecked and is really vigorous.

Pruned back to shape but the lower branches have been left to grow further to thicken and also strengthen the weakest part of the tree. (Most trees are apical dominant.)

you are leaving at least one bud further behind on each branch you prune. This includes any buds on remaining side branches.

For those of you wishing to develop, refine and improve your bonsai, you will find much more detailed advice on pruning and training techniques in Chapters 7 and 8 of this book.

This *Juniperus procumbens* is becoming more like a bush than a tree.

Now the foliage clouds and spaces are clearly defined and the underlying branch structure is visible, making it much more like a tree again.

Established junipers with juvenile, needle-type foliage can be kept in shape by pinching.

This *Pinus mugo* has extended really well and had a good season's growth.

Junipers with adult, scale-like foliage can be allowed to extend at the tips and then pruned back to the tree's profile with scissors.

Even before we remove some of the older and downward-pointing needles, there is more light and air in the canopy, whilst the tree's underlying branch structure is now visible.

Larch extensions can be shortened by pinching in summer and then more detailed pruning can be carried out in December when the tree is in its bare winter image.

Case Study: Trident Maple (Affectionately Known as 'Big John')

February 2002 – I acquired this tree in March 2000 after its importation from Korea. It was a bare stump with not a single branch when I started. The bread tray it sits comfortably in gives you an indication of size.

November 2002 – branches have been allowed to grow freely, especially the lower branches, which we need to thicken up. The taper on this heavy stump is simply amazing.

May 2003 – the initial, unchecked flush of early season's growth. Now, as the leaves mature and the growth spurt reaches its climax, we can intervene, make a selection and cut back unwanted branches.

May 2004 – Following a similar flush of growth to what we had in 2003, shoots have been cut back to keep the upper area of the tree in check. The lower branches have been wired out and allowed to extend further. In ensuing years, branches will be selected and grown to form a larger, more appropriate canopy.

May 2014 – once again, strong early season growth covered the now massive canopy of foliage. We work down the tree cutting back long shoots and removing the outer leaves but leaving new internal shoots untouched.

June 2014 – exactly one month after the last picture and look at all the new growth the tree is producing. This new growth will be more strictly controlled as we start to build good ramification.

March 2015 – all that new top growth has naturally resulted in a similar amount of new root growth in the pot, so time for repotting. This is a typical, healthy, dense, fibrous root system associated with trident maples.

8

October 2015 – after all his hard work, finally the tree gets a chance to show off at a national bonsai exhibition. The leaves are a good, uniform size, the soil surface has been mossed up and the bark is ageing nicely.

9

March 2018 – another repotting is completed and the tree is soundly back in the pot with some fresh compost. This picture also shows how far we have progressed with the ramification of fine twigs.

10

May 2020 – once again that first flush of growth is complete, leaves are becoming larger and the tree almost resembles a bush. New shoots are just starting to extend.

11

May 2020 – the new shoots are trimmed back to the first short internode. Most of the outer leaves, especially the bigger ones, will be removed, but any new shoots and leaves inside the tree will be left untouched.

12

Right: June 2020 – exactly one month later and all the red new shoots and buds are clearly visible. The green leaves are the ones we left on a month ago. I am keeping the tree contained but increasing ramification at the same time.

CHAPTER 6

REPOTTING
Root Considerations and Problems

Introduction

I briefly introduced you to the task of repotting in the previous two chapters on indoor and outdoor bonsai. I maintain that the best time to repot your tree is just as it is about to enter into a period of new growth following a period of dormancy (this is usually spring for most trees), and that we try and leave a reasonable period of time in between repottings (around four years).

The Bonsai Pot

Bonsai pots come in all sizes, different shapes and colours. Normally, when you acquire a tree, you also inherit the pot that it sits in. The pot has to provide the right conditions for the tree to grow in and must also give it stability. It is imperative that there are adequate drainage holes in the base of the pot and for outdoor trees in cooler climates, the pot also needs to be frost-proof. In addition to the horticultural aspect, there are aesthetic considerations too; ideally, the tree and pot should be the perfect marriage. It is not unlike trying to find the right frame for a painting or photograph.

Generally, conifers look good in unglazed pots, whilst coloured-glazed pots can be used to complement the seasonal display of flowers or fruit and autumn colours associated with deciduous trees. Beauty is in the eye of the beholder and you are the one who has to look at the tree on a daily basis, so you are the one who makes the final decision. Mass-produced ceramic pots are imported from China and Japan, whilst there are many excellent bonsai potters in Europe who will make you a bespoke pot specifically designed for your tree. Cheaper frost-proof, heavy-duty, plastic pots are available for the trees you have in training that are not yet ready for pride of place on your display bench. I will discuss the aesthetics of bonsai pot selection in more detail in Chapter 9 under 'Bonsai Aesthetics'.

No matter how many pots I have in stock, it still proves difficult to find the right one in exactly the desired shape, size and colour.

In cultivating our bonsai we are diligently providing water as required and feeding on a regular basis to encourage our trees to be healthy and to grow as strongly as possible. The by-product of this is that the tree will grow roots – lots of them! Eventually, the roots will reach the inner walls of the pot and start to encircle the rootball. The roots at the bottom of the pot can, in time, form a solid mass that can inhibit drainage and lead to problems of root rot. The compost itself will gradually break down to a powdery form and be washed out of the pot or may contribute to drainage problems. One of the benefits of akadama, the Japanese bonsai soil, is that it breaks down slowly over time, creating more space in which new roots can grow. I have repotted trees imported from Japan and found the pots to be filled almost entirely with roots and no evidence of compost whatsoever.

You can see that the repotting of trees on a regular basis is a very important aspect of bonsai cultivation. If trees are not repotted, then eventually they will start to deteriorate, weaken and can die. Repotting is not just about replacing and replenishing the soil. The art of bonsai involves creating and refining the most amazing image of a tree in miniature. At the same time we have to produce and maintain a compact healthy rootball capable of supporting and sustaining the developing tree.

Repotting Method

This step-by-step guide illustrates the basic approach to repotting a bonsai tree. The subject tree is a *Pseudolarix* imported from China. The need for this repot was brought about because the existing pot had been damaged, but you can also see that the rootball was becoming very compacted.

Repotting Method

Step 1: The buds are colouring and swelling, so we need to repot before they burst open. The necessary tools are close to hand – scissors and pruning shears, chopstick for working the roots and soil, pliers and wire-cutters, soil scoop.

Step 2: The new pot with mesh cut to fit over the drainage holes. The client wanted a pot of similar colour and this is approximately the same size but a different shape.

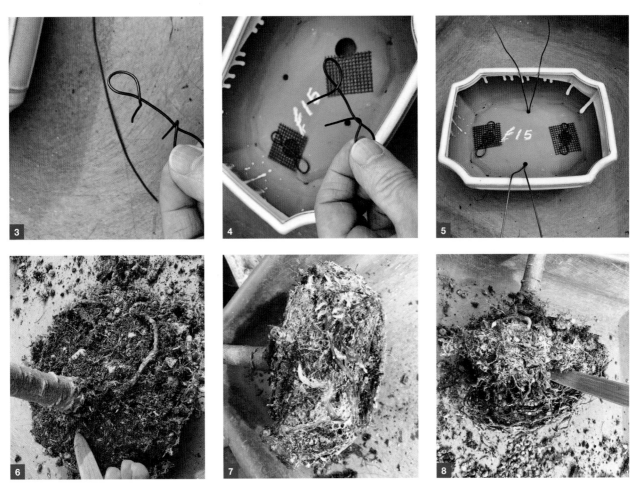

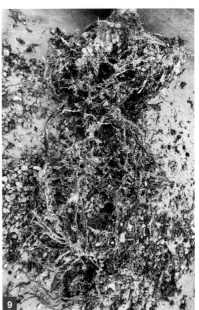

Repotting Method (cont'd)

Step 3: A piece of thin, 1.5mm, aluminium bonsai wire is cut and bent to form a butterfly clip, which is then used to secure the mesh into the bonsai pot.

Step 4: The wires are pushed through the mesh and through the drainage holes. The projecting wires below the pot are then folded back flush with the pot to secure the mesh.

Step 5: Two longer pieces of 2mm aluminium bonsai wire are passed under the pot and through the smaller holes. These will be used to secure the tree into the pot. If smaller tie-wire holes have not been provided, then you will have to use the drainage holes.

Step 6: Any tie wires are cut below the pot so that the tree can be removed from its existing pot. Work from the trunk outwards to carefully remove any surface debris, weeds and perished compost.

Step 7: The presence of white mycorrhiza fungus is evidence of a healthy root system, as it enjoys a symbiotic relationship with the roots. Any old pieces of mesh can be removed from the rootball.

Step 8: Now we can use the chopstick or a rake to gently comb and tease out the roots from this tight tangled mess. The fresh, brown, white-tipped roots are another sign of good health.

Step 9: Once the roots are combed out, you can see by their length just how much they must have circled the pot, congesting and compacting the rootball.

Repotting Method (cont'd)

Step 10: The thicker, combed-out, elongated roots can now be cut back with scissors. To avoid any transference of disease, I use an older pair of scissors for pruning roots and keep my better scissors for branch/twig pruning.

Step 11: The reduced rootball ready for going back in the pot. As much thin fibrous root as possible is retained near the trunk and soil/roots around the base of the trunk have been left untouched to minimize shock/disturbance.

Step 12: Compost is mounded in the centre of the pot ready for the tree's placement. The pot was prepared beforehand to minimize the amount of time the exposed roots are left open and vulnerable to drying out.

Step 13: The tie wires can now be brought over the rootball and tightened/twisted together to secure the tree in the pot. Try and tighten over an edge of the rootball or thick root to avoid the wires snapping as you twist them.

Step 14: Gently push the tree slightly away from you as you work the compost into the roots and under the rootball. This will firm the tree in and avoid any air pockets.

Step 15: The finished tree planted just off-centre, so that it looks more natural. The canopy should sit nicely balanced over the pot. Make sure you decide on the front of the tree and align it correctly before finally securing it to the pot.

Compost

Ingredients

Akadama

This is a naturally occurring clay-like substance graded into different-sized particles and imported already bagged from Japan. There are a large number of types of akadama available in Japan but the one imported for bonsai use is a double-line brand, which signifies being of harder quality; it won't break down as easily. It is capable of taking up moisture and holding it, giving the roots time to absorb the water and any nutrients that you have introduced. It is granular and free-draining, breaking down very slowly, which then creates more spaces for new roots to grow into. The fact that the colour darkens when it is moist and becomes lighter as it dries can help in determining when the tree needs watering again.

Kanuma

This is another Japanese soil very similar to akadama but is very light in weight by comparison and a pale yellow colour in its dry state. It behaves very similarly to akadama but is used almost exclusively for Satsuki azaleas.

Kiryu

This is a Japanese soil that I encounter less frequently in Europe but is sometimes used in compost mixes for pines. It often looks coarser than akadama and is more yellow in colour compared with the brown colour of akadama. The downside of the Japanese soils is that they can appear to be costly and are only generally available online or from specialist bonsai nurseries.

Pumice

This is a volcanic residue that is white in colour and light in weight. It is available in different-graded particle sizes. Each granule is full of capillaries that take up water and then gradually release it. It acts like a natural filtration system within your compost. It helps keep the compost open and does not readily break down.

Bims

This is a river gravel that originated in Germany and we have successfully used it in our bonsai compost mixes for many years. Again, it is a greyish white in colour, capable of holding water and does not break down.

The double-line brand akadama signifies harder quality, having been mined from a greater depth.

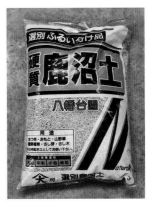

Kanuma is a much lighter and paler compost used for Satsuki azaleas.

Horticultural Aggregate

I have recently started using this in my bonsai composts and the results have been encouraging. This is made up of small, black beads and is generally light in weight, especially when dry. This blends in well when mixed with akadama and avoids the stark-white appearance of compost mixes using pumice or bims. I understand that this product is also used successfully under greens on golf courses.

Peat/Modern Alternatives

In my early bonsai years when akadama was not as readily available, bonsai mixes tended to be based on peat or garden loam. If you do decide to use soil-based compost, some of the modern alternatives to peat may be worth trying, especially if they offer a similar craggy and coarse consistency. Avoid using general seed and potting composts because the particle sizes here are too fine and they will soon clog and block drainage holes. Some people use composted forest bark as an alternative to peat but this can be very dusty and dries out too quickly.

This is a river gravel called bims, similar in appearance and performance to pumice.

Horticultural aggregate sometimes listed for sale as kurodama.

Grit

This is another ingredient from my early bonsai years. A horticultural or alpine grit up to a particle size of around 4mm can help with drainage and keeping a compost mix open.

Cat Litter

Yes, you did read this correctly! I must confess this is something I have never used but you may come across it on your bonsai travels. I understand that there are only certain brands that are suitable as bonsai compost material. I have had cats most of my life and the cat litters I used helped to bind the mess together to make it easier to remove and dispose of. This property is the last thing you want in bonsai compost, as it will soon impair good drainage. I also worry about any chemicals that may have been introduced by the manufacturers to combat odour.

Moler

This is an excavated product, which is then manufactured and used to provide insulation bricks for the building industry. It is light and has a high natural clay content, which is why I believe some people have experimented with it as a cheaper alternative to akadama. The compost material takes the form of reddish-brown balls of different sizes. Once again, it is not a product I have used personally.

The Right Mix?

The world of bonsai composts is much akin to the world of champion vegetable growers. Every enthusiast you encounter will no doubt have their own secret mix and

This is a mix I currently use for conifers and is 50 per cent akadama and 50 per cent horticultural aggregate. Notice how granular good bonsai compost should be.

each one will undoubtedly claim that theirs is the best. Look at their trees; if they are strong and healthy, then maybe it is worth considering; if they look a bit weak or yellow instead of green, then maybe their compost is not so good.

It might be worth checking with your nearest specialist bonsai nursery to see what they recommend and what seems to work in the local environment.

The compost mix you use must be capable of physically and nutritionally supporting the tree. It should drain freely and contain oxygen in the form of air. It should be able to remain damp without becoming waterlogged, retaining its physical state for as long as possible to reduce any tendency to compact. Also within its properties should be a 'buffer' capable of reserving nutrients in a dissolved state. Enthusiasts will continue to experiment to find a satisfactory solution based on the availability of ingredients locally. Hence the importance of understanding the requirements of a good bonsai compost.

The mixes I use are heavily based on akadama. The Japanese have been growing bonsai in akadama for centuries and if there was something better, I think they would have found it by now. For deciduous trees I use three parts akadama to one part pumice (bims or horticultural aggregate could be used instead). I also use this mix for the indoor trees. For coniferous trees I want a more free-draining soil, so I use 50 per cent akadama and 50 per cent pumice.

If you are unable to acquire these materials and are restricted to what your local garden centre has to offer, then I would use something like a 50 per cent peat alternative to 50 per cent grit as a general compost for your bonsai. You could always increase the peat content slightly for deciduous trees if you wanted to increase moisture retention. I have also found this mix works well for trees in their early years of cultivation, which may have been lifted from the ground and placed in slightly larger training pots. It is certainly a cheaper option at this stage of development.

Just remember that the compost is the only thing you really give to the tree, so give it the best you can afford. I can never understand why some enthusiasts will pay hundreds or thousands of pounds for a tree and then buy a sack of cat litter rather than akadama to save a few pounds! Trust me, it really is false economy. If the compost is wrong and the tree is suffering, then all our other training techniques are basically a waste of time.

This Satsuki azalea is clearly struggling, with evidence of dieback and very little weak new growth. Flowers have been incorrectly removed, leaving seed pods to develop.

Brown and yellowing tips on the leaves and poor growth can be an indication that there is a problem with the roots and that the tree is being kept too wet.

A heavy, continuous moss growth on the soil surface and trunk, often accompanied by weed growth and a blackened surface texture, is a good indication that the compost is too wet.

When the tree is lifted from the pot, the compost is a soggy mess with little evidence of new outward root growth from the rootball.

Problems and Considerations

Too Wet

We have already discussed how the apparently simple task of watering bonsai can be very difficult to master. Some enthusiasts, and especially newcomers to the hobby, can be too conscientious and so determined that their trees will not dry out that they go to the other extreme and keep their trees too wet. Just to be on the safe side, some people may even water their trees every day, regardless of weather conditions and without actually checking the condition of the compost. In trying to avoid one problem, you can be inadvertently creating another one that can have serious consequences. Wet soil can become compacted, break

down more quickly and block drainage holes, which just exacerbates the problem. Roots become too wet, dieback and eventually rot back into the rootball.

Too Dry

During each repot, whilst we have removed soil from below and around the edges, most of the central core of the rootball around the trunk is left intact. Over a period of time, with the constant wetting and then drying out of the soil, this established section of the rootball can become extremely solid. When you water the tree it is almost like you are trying to get water to pass through solid concrete and, inevitably, most of the water just runs off the pot instead of penetrating the rootball. I have lifted trees out of pots shortly after

A closer inspection of the upper area shows weak growth and a lot of dieback especially to the small inner branches.

You can see how solid the central area of the rootball is compared with the outer area of fresher compost. The tree is not getting enough water in the lower section of the pot.

Satsuki azaleas are naturally stronger in their lower side-branches and weaker at the apex, but here the disparity is a little too obvious.

With trees like this you have to regularly make holes into the solid rootball using a screwdriver or metal chopstick to help water penetrate the central root area.

watering and found the lower section of the rootball to be so dry that it looks like the tree has not been watered for weeks. If you have a tree like this you may have to water it several times during your normal routine watering session. The initial watering will wet the soil and make it easier for the roots to absorb water from the subsequent watering. In severe cases, you may have to periodically submerge the whole pot in a tub of water for, say, five minutes to ensure that the whole rootball becomes adequately wet.

Weeds

It is important to keep the soil in the pot free of weeds and it is much easier to remove them when they first appear, rather than to let them get firmly established. If the weeds

are allowed to develop, they will take full advantage of the water and food you are applying, which is intended for the tree. Apart from looking unsightly, they can cause drainage problems, inhibit the growth of the tree and, in severe cases, lead to the tree's demise.

Root Rot

Sometimes the appearance of the tree can lead you to believe that all is well. Growth may have been a little less vigorous than in the past with only moderate branch extension but leaf colour and condition can appear to be normal. It is often in the spring when the problems begin to emerge, as the tree fails to leaf out or is often struggling to grow and is very weak. It needs strong, healthy roots to

Some small grasses can look natural but they take over the pot and are then almost impossible to eradicate because they can regrow from the tiniest fragment of tissue left behind.

This can look like a healthy root system but all the fine white roots are from weeds not the tree. A solid mat like this is formed on the base of the pot, which then blocks drainage leading to roots becoming too wet and rotting

This Antarctic birch (*Nothofagus antarctica*) looks fine with developing twiggy growth. Only the extensive moss growth suggests that the compost may have been on the wet side.

On removal from the pot, the tree leaves the compost far too easily, leaving virtually all the compost and dead, now unattached, rotted roots behind.

The soil-based compost was too heavy and had remained wet for far too long. The compost has eventually dried out but the damage was done, and then it can be very difficult to get it evenly and adequately wet again.

suddenly engage after a dormant winter and push the tree forwards. The tree's demise may have started during the last growing season, but it plodded along on built-up reserves until a long, cold, wet winter finally takes its toll.

A Cry for Help

I have had students bring their trees to a class, marvelling enthusiastically about how amazing it looks – but sometimes all is not what it seems. A well-developed pine may have very small needles in scale with the branches. Are the needles small because of good cultivation and ramification techniques or are they small because the tree is struggling and there is a problem with the roots?

Have you ever seen such a large amount of fruit on such a small tree – it looks brilliant. Is the excessive amount of fruit this year down to your feeding programme/good husbandry and this year's seasonal climate changes or is the tree feeling threatened and desperately trying to perpetuate itself by producing as much seed as possible? So, before you start patting yourself on the back and reaching for the camera, just look at the bigger picture and take

This Japanese white pine was struggling and needed repotting. Compare the needle length with one taken from a similar healthy white pine growing normally.

These cones were removed from a larch bonsai prior to carrying out a repotting, which was desperately needed.

stock of the tree itself. When was the tree last repotted? Has the tree had any growing issues during the past couple of years? Has it dried out or been too wet? What does the compost look like? Maybe you need to just lift the tree out of the pot at the earliest safe opportunity to make sure everything is alright.

Rejuvenating a Tired Tree

After years of growing in a small, shallow pot, some trees can really show signs of stress and become very weak. They may put on hardly any new growth. Branch extension may be so minimal as to be hardly noticeable. Leaves become very small. Unexplained dieback on shoots and whole branches can occur, especially on those inside the canopy where they are not getting enough light.

Sometimes potting the tree into a larger 'growing' pot for a couple of seasons can make all the difference. In this period you are more interested in growth and vigour, rather than appearance and refinement of image. You have to maintain some control because you don't want to lose the delicate structure the tree may have built up over the years. You may be able to let some of the weaker lower branches extend to build up their stature, whilst keeping the twigs around the apex under control. Some sacrifice branches may be allowed to extend to create vigour and strength prior to being removed when the tree is returned to its 'show' pot.

In extreme cases I have returned some good-quality bonsai into the ground in a growing bed for a couple of years and the results have been amazing. Some struggling trees, which I may otherwise have lost, not only recovered well, but became stronger and much better trees afterwards.

General Improvement

In addition to maintaining a healthy root system to support and nourish the tree, you are also trying to improve the structure and appearance of the roots over a period of time. The tree enjoys a sheltered and cherished existence in a pot and, with a 'bonsai servant' on tap, doesn't need massive roots to firmly anchor it to the ground, as it would in the wild. Over a period of time we are gradually replacing the heavier roots with fine, fibrous, feeder roots to fully nourish the tree. We also try to improve the nebari, the root flare at the base of the trunk, and expose any heavy, neat, outward-growing roots on the soil surface to enhance the tree's natural appearance and provide visual balance. We are aiming for a radial arrangement of uncrossing roots growing outwards towards the edge of the pot. Because we may only expose the root system every four or five years it is important that when we do, we try to improve it as much as possible without causing any additional undue stress to the tree.

This specimen maple is pictured on the frontispiece to this book in its full autumn glory. After losing vigour and a few branches, I transferred it to this large, deeper, mica pot. After a few years in here the tree was growing stronger than when it arrived from Japan and with improved ramification.

Case Study: Japanese White Pine – the Soil of the Inner Sanctum

Left: This white pine has become 'leggy' and is ready for some wiring and styling. The needles are very small with little evidence of new growth extension from the previous season.

The soil surface looks very compacted and the soil of the inner rootball around the base of the trunk is black, unlike the akadama soil around the edges. We need to investigate further.

The exterior of the rootball is solid but in reasonable condition. There are healthy, brown, white-tipped roots and some mycorrhiza is present. The tree does not appear to have been getting enough water.

The inner soil and roots are in poor condition. If we do a normal repot and remove the healthy outer roots, we will only have weak roots remaining. To bare root the tree completely could put the tree's life at risk.

5

6

We need to carefully remove the soil of the inner rootball without damaging any of the roots in this area. A large section of the outer rootball is left intact with no disturbance.

The soil removed from this inner area is poor, powdery, black and contains dead roots and tufts of matted, perished roots. A combination of poor drainage and poor soil has caused some of the roots to rot.

The underneath and outer edges of the rootball have also become so solid that they are inhibiting the natural drainage of the compost. They are carefully removed without disturbing the section of outer roots that we need to keep intact.

7

8

9

The tree is now ready for placing back in the pot with some fresh compost. The problem areas have been dealt with but a large area of strong, healthy roots has been left untouched to minimize stress and keep the tree alive.

The tree after the repotting with fresh compost added below, around and inside the rootball. After two growing seasons, the rootball can be re-examined and, if sufficient new roots have grown in the inner sanctum, then a normal repot can be carried out.

CHAPTER 7

TRUNKS AND
MAIN BRANCHES

Introduction

At the beginning of Chapter 3, I talked about buying an established bonsai at the size you want, rather than expecting a small bonsai to grow into a much larger one. We can greatly refine and improve the image of the bonsai and, whilst its girth and silhouette will increase gradually over time, our training techniques and the confinement in the pot will certainly stop it doubling in size. If you want the

The thin branches on this collected hawthorn stump are totally out of character with the heavy trunk and will need to be grown much thicker to complement the character of the tree.

The thin, tight branches of this juniper follow the slender, meandering movement in the trunk and are in keeping with the tree's literati-style character.

larger tree, save up your money and buy it – don't purchase the cheaper, smaller tree expecting it to become the larger one.

When you are starting out with a new tree, try to acquire the tree/trunk size you want or be prepared to grow-on a smaller piece of material in to the trunk size you really want before styling and developing branches.

It is also important to appreciate that the character of the trunk will set the tone of the tree, influencing the size/shape of the canopy and its underlying branch structure. Once you have acquired or grown a desirable trunk, then you will have to design and grow the branches to complement it. If you acquire an established bonsai you can examine the existing branch structure and then take steps to improve and refine what you already have.

I think that in Japan the initial styling is regarded very much as just a beginning, a start for the new tree. Main branches are selected, wired and often bent down into the desired position whilst their side branches are simply spread open to receive maximum light and air. This transformation may be fairly basic and uninspiring, but creates a very natural framework for the proposed tree. The open foliage clouds are then encouraged to back-bud and achieve greater density more quickly with appropriate cultivation techniques.

In the West the initial styling is excitingly viewed as a spectacular event, especially at bonsai shows where a long leggy piece of garden material is somehow miraculously transformed into an almost finished looking bonsai. This work often involves substantial wiring and some serious manipulation of branches. The existing foliage has been crowded together to form a foliage canopy which often inhibits new bud development. When the wire is removed the long leggy branches are often unable to support themselves, and return to dangling freely.

In my early bonsai years I attended many workshops and when we styled a bonsai out of a piece of raw material, it was a case of simply trying to get the best tree design out of the available branches you had. When we style trees today, sometimes our design is based on small shoots or buds that we will grow into the branches we need. The immediate instant bonsai image may not have the same impact but, ultimately, the developed shoots/buds will generally result in a more natural-looking, denser bonsai that is easier to refine and develop further.

The underlying basic principles discussed in this chapter can be applied to both deciduous and coniferous trees.

Growing Up

In Chapter 2 we discussed sources of material, including young plants from your garden. In Chapter 3 we explained how material could be grown-on either in a pot or in the ground until you reached the desired size of trunk. Now we can look at how to improve the trunk line and create branches, using the trident maple example shown here.

Original growth in the ground cut back to a suitable side shoot

1

My student Andrew had grown this trident on to increase the diameter of the trunk and improve its nebari at the base. The trunk had been cut back to a suitable side shoot, which had then been allowed to grow unchecked as a new leader.

2

The side shoot had thickened well to provide good taper and movement leading from the original trunk.

The side shoot is now cut back to another side shoot sprouting in the opposite direction.

This close up shows another proposed change in the trunk line and the presence of more buds around the trunk.

Seen from the other side, the new shoot is allowed to extend as before to thicken and create good taper.

This process is repeated so that we now have a short trunk with excellent taper, character and movement.

Emerging buds were now allowed to grow freely and some of the lower branches were loosely wired into position.

The branches are now all pruned back and we are beginning to establish the basic shape of the tree.

Left: The tree is again encouraged to become vigorous to further develop the branches.

Right: The basic form is complete with good trunk movement, some heavy, low branches and finer shoots around the apex. New growth will now be much more tightly controlled to create ramification and fine twigs.

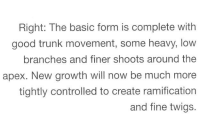

Reducing Down

This process was briefly discussed in Chapter 2 when detailing how you could source potential bonsai raw material from your own garden. Large shrubs and trees often have to be removed from where they are growing because they have outgrown their space or the area is required for an alternative use. Most of the branches will be removed, as they are unlikely to be useable in our new tree design, but some heavy, low branches may have value, whilst a substantial higher branch may be adopted as a new leader to improve the line and taper of the trunk. You will then be left with a hefty stump upon which you can grow branches to create a very old-looking, impressive bonsai. I dug a purple maple out of my garden, which was then purchased by another student called Andrew, and together we continued with its development.

April 2013 – this *Acer palmatum* had suffered some serious dieback in the past and was now outgrowing its allotted space so I decided to remove it.

Existing branches have been pruned back to take pressure off the tree. The rootball has been reduced and fibrous root retained to fit the allocated training pot.

May 2013 – the tree has leafed out and is growing well with its attractive early season red colour. It will be allowed to grow freely to help it recover from the transplant.

November 2013 – all the season's growth has now been cut back to short stumps. The natural deadwood, an attractive ageing feature, has also been reduced.

June 2014 – more unchecked growth to sustain the vigour and strength of the tree, which is seen here in its summer green colour.

The growth is once again pruned back but this time with an initial branch selection. A strong shoot at the top will continue with the trunk line and taper.

November 2016 – lower side-branches have been allowed to grow long to thicken, whilst the apex has been controlled for tighter shoots and better ramification.

After pruning, the lower shoots are left long. They emerge from the original pruned stumps in a more natural horizontal line to promote an older image.

November 2017 – having been allowed to grow the lower branches continue to thicken and are shaping up well, whilst the apex is also starting to widen and develop.

After pruning back. In a short time my student Andrew has become really accomplished at carving and the hollowed-out trunk instantly adds character and a sense of greater age.

May 2018 – the tree has been repotted into a larger pot and is now producing amazing new growth. The lengthening branches continue to thicken.

After pruning back to shape. We have pruned some longer branches back to a stronger side shoot, which will extend faster and continue the thickening process.

October 2018 – the extent of the season's growth is more clearly visible now, as the tree does its best to please us with some good autumn colours.

Right: After pruning, and the silhouette of an ageing tree is at last beginning to emerge. Pruning around the base of the tree over the years has improved the exposed roots.

October 2019 – the remnants of shoots pruned throughout the growing season are clearly visible as we exert greater control on branch extension.

After pruning and some cleaning out of the canopy. A plausible basic framework of branches has been established and now refinement can begin.

The merging of the white pine upper trunk and the black pine lower trunk is unnatural and exaggerated, whilst the upward emergence of the main branch at ninety degrees is clumsy.

Tilting the trunk slightly enables us to shape the branches more in the semi-cascade style, making it easier to link the lower and upper areas, whilst creating a much more natural image.

Design Considerations

Trunk Angle

Don't take for granted that how the tree currently stands is its definitive permanent posture. This applies to trees being removed from the ground, stumps in training boxes and established bonsai in ceramic pots. Be prepared to prop the tree up at different angles and view it from different sides; you may be surprised by what you see. Sometimes the whole character of the tree can dramatically change just by being positioned at a different angle and viewed from a different side, with the branches adjusted accordingly. A change of angle may result in branches that were gently sloping down naturally, now frantically reaching for the sky and greatly distorting the trees image.

The Japanese white pine featured in these images was brought to me by a client for wiring and restyling. The change brought about by simply changing the planting angle was quite extraordinary.

Apical Dominance

Most trees tend to be apical dominant, the top being the most vigorous part of the tree where branches race to the

After wiring and styling, I was so pleased with the transformation and how this humble white pine had been elevated to a whole new level. Thankfully my client was pleased too!

sky totally unencumbered and having unrestricted access to natural light. Branches below are shaded by the branches above and often have to fight with each other for any available light and air flow. Inner branches become weaker and die, whilst outer branches extend at the tips desperately searching for light. This might work out alright in nature, with the tree basically growing bigger and bigger, doing all

'Well you did say let them grow!' The canopy of this privet bonsai has been kept tightly under control allowing the vigour to be concentrated in lengthening the lower branches.

You can see how thick these lower branches have become by allowing them to grow unchecked and how they are thickening where they emerge from the trunk.

The thickened branches are cut back to the profile of the tree. Now we can concentrate on growing secondary branches and twigs on them to create foliage clouds.

In addition to allowing the low branches to extend, a branch at the top had also been allowed to grow unchecked to create taper and side branches to form the apex.

it needs to do to stay alive and flourish. Unfortunately, we have to burden our bonsai with aesthetic and design considerations, which inhibit its natural freedom. We need the tree to grow to remain healthy but we need to keep it compact and small. In creating a mature tree image, we need fine twigs in the naturally strong apical area and heavy, vigorous branches in the weaker, lower area. We have to control nature and reverse this natural growth pattern by keeping the upper areas of the tree under tighter control and allowing the lower branches to extend unchecked until they have reached the desired girth. When you allow a lower branch to extend, you need to cut back any side shoots to the first bud so that the growth is concentrated on extending the length of the branch, which will also cause it to thicken at its base. Allowing side shoots to extend will result in thickening at these junctions along the branch, rather than concentrating the thickening at the point where the branch emerges from the trunk.

Trunk Taper

When considering the line of the trunk from the base to what will be the apex, you are looking for good taper and, unless the tree is very formal, some nice movement. Once you find the most desirable trunk line, it will make it easier to select the main branches. You are looking for heavier branches in the lower section of the tree but then thinner branches as you progress towards the apex. You will then know which branches you need to grow to get thicker and which areas of the tree you need to keep under control to restrict any thickening growth. To create or improve the taper it may be necessary to let a side or top branch extend to thicken and create a smooth even flow from the lower trunk into the area from which we will grow the apex.

Left: This cedar bonsai had grown too strong to the side and become very flat, spoiling the trunk line and having no clearly defined apex.

Right: The strong side-growth is cut back to create some interesting deadwood and the strongest branch is wired upwards to continue the trunk line, to provide a recognizable apex and to greatly improve the whole image of the tree.

Established Bonsai

When you acquire an established bonsai, the trunk line and style have usually been already determined and may be what attracted you to the tree in the first place. There will also be an abundance of branches that should be giving you a pleasing image. Just how good this basic structure and the tree's image are will no doubt have been reflected in the price you paid to acquire it. Generally speaking, when you buy a bonsai, you are often buying time. In theory you will be paying much more for a tree imported from Japan if someone has already invested forty or fifty years in its development, rather than one that has only been in training for, say, ten to fifteen years. Hence the reason that good-quality specimen bonsai can be seriously expensive. You will never buy a 'finished' bonsai. As we stated previously, unlike other art forms, with bonsai there is a beginning but never an end. The tree has life itself and continues to grow, develop and evolve.

You have to carefully study your new acquisition and assess how you can improve it. Can I improve the nebari and exposed roots at the base of the trunk? Is the trunk line and taper satisfactory? Do the main branches need growing stronger or do some branches need to be removed? Is the apex and overall silhouette of the tree satisfactory? There will always be scope to improve on the ramification of finer branches and twigs. Is there a better front or planting angle? It doesn't matter how good your best tree looks, I can assure you that it will always be possible to take it to another higher level.

This *Acer palmatum* has reasonable taper and movement and is a good basic image. The lower branches have been allowed to extend to become the heaviest on the tree.

A stocky trunked Korean hornbeam with some ramification and twigs, but the lower branches need to be heavier to complement the bulk in the trunk.

Case Study: *Taxus baccata* Hedging Material

Above: July 2016 – this tree was dug out of a hedge at the end of 2014 and potted up with little foliage remaining. Eighteen months later and the tree has recovered well.

Top right: March 2017 – the tree continued to grow until my student Rob brought it back into the studio for an initial branch selection, which you can see in this picture.

Right: October 2017 – the selected branches have extended and some of the original pruning stumps have been shortened and marked for further deadwood creation.

Bark has been removed and a shari created. The original heavy trunk has been torn back to look more natural and to create an illusion of taper.

September 2018 – the tree has benefited from a repotting and put on some good growth. The stumps have been hollowed-out to create a more natural older look.

After another branch selection. Two branches were competing to become the new leader and so the higher one was removed.

September 2019 – the tree continues to grow well. The new leader and some lower branches have been allowed to extend to thicken up.

The extending branches have been cut back to strong side-shoots to promote taper and to encourage more back-budding.

September 2020 – the tree is becoming much denser, the main branches are thickening well and we have good material from which to select the structure of the tree.

The Use of Deadwood and Carving

I discussed earlier in this chapter the idea of using larger, older material that we could reduce in size to create a substantial and mature bonsai image. This can lead to problems, with the lower section of the trunk that we want to use being very heavy and with no taper. Sometimes we can grow a new leader and trunk line to give convincing taper. Where this is not possible, we may have to use carving techniques to hollow out a trunk to disguise or hide the lack of taper and to camouflage large pruning cuts.

Example 1: *Taxus baccata*

This sequence of photos is another example of my student Andrew's excellent carving work, which I referred to earlier in this chapter. This is a tall tree and the foliage will be arranged close to the trunk with a narrow spread to emphasize the height.

July 2017 – the separating trunks in the upper section are now more clearly visible. A wide shari has been initiated, which extends into a projecting root.

May 2017 – this large *Taxus baccata* is almost multi-trunked and with very little taper. The growth is strong but thin and growing in an upwards direction.

Bark has been stripped off the upper sections. The trunk with the shari has now been hollowed-out from the front. Branches have also been thinned out.

September 2018 – the carving has been extremely well refined. Now we have drama, character and the image of a large old tree struggling to survive.

October 2019 – the tree has grown well. Branches have thickened and have now been wired ready for the tree to have its first styling.

Branches are brought down and arranged around the trunk. Now we can develop more side branches and create foliage clouds and spaces.

April 2016 – an innocuous overgrown privet bush planted in an uninspiring green bucket. Not the most encouraging start for an aspiring bonsai.

When the foliage is pruned back and the planting angle is changed, there might just be a glimmer of hope, but there are serious problems to overcome.

Example 2: Privet

My student Keith's privet was dominated by the heavy remains of the obviously chopped trunk. It will need seriously hollowing out to try to camouflage the cut and produce a convincing tree-like image. This will be a squat, powerful tree and, therefore, needs an overall foliage canopy that will be as wide as it is tall.

Right: September 2017 – a new pot and replanted at the new angle. The problems of the heavy stumps are being dealt with by extensive carving/hollowing-out.

Branches are selected and pruned accordingly whilst more detail is added to the carving work.

Right: October 2019 – the tree has continued to grow strongly. Branches have been allowed to extend to thicken and then pruned back. We are now developing more side shoots.

A close-up shows the main branches have been wired into place, whilst detailed attention to the carving makes it appear more natural. This work will continue.

CHAPTER 8

SECONDARY BRANCHES AND TWIGS

Introduction

I remember a story about a lady bringing a small oak tree to a bonsai class with just a couple of huge leaves on it. Her only concern with the tree was how she could get the leaf size down and in scale with the thin trunk. The basic problem was not so much the size of the leaf but the fact that there were only two of them! If you try to imagine that the tree needs a certain size of surface area of the leaves to grow and survive, then the larger the number of leaves to provide this surface area the smaller they will be. If you concentrate your efforts on growing more branches and twigs, then to a large degree the size of the leaves and needles will take care of themselves. Bonsai enthusiasts often get obsessed with leaf/needle size in young trees they are just starting up with. When students arrive with trees in the early years of training, with large leaves or needles, I am delighted because this translates to me as strong health and vigour. We can use this energy to get to where we want to be more quickly, to move the tree forward and take it to its next level.

Right: Compare this picture of my privet bonsai taken in March 2015 with the picture of the tree from 2001 in Chapter 2, under the section 'Plant Material from the Garden'.

Start by making a study of your tree and assessing the underlying branch structure. For deciduous trees, this is best done in the winter months when you can see exactly what you have and how good the tree is. A well-developed deciduous bonsai will look better in its bare winter image than in its dense, concealing, summer canopy. Decide where you need thicker main branches, extra secondary branches and more fine twigs. This will then provide you with a cultivation plan for the coming growing season. This chapter will help you in the implementation of such a plan.

Design Considerations

Style, Position and Branch Angle

How we develop our branch structure will be influenced by the style and size of the tree and the position of the branch on the tree. A tall forest conifer may have short branches with foliage quite close to the trunk, which will accentuate the tree's height. A short tree with a powerful, stocky trunk will have heavy, low branches and may be wider than it is tall. A mature deciduous tree image will have a broad, conical shape, with a well-rounded, wide crown. Our branches

will follow the rhythm of the trunk and maintain this rhythm throughout the branch framework. A formal, straight trunk will be accompanied by straight branches, perhaps with a gentle meandering flow from the trunk to the outer canopy. If we have a trunk with lots of movement, then our branches will have lots of movement too. Our image reflects nature and the fact that trunk and branches are growing in the same environment and will react to the prevailing conditions in the same way.

Following on from our design discussions in Chapter 7, we have established that the lowest branches represent the oldest branches on the tree and, therefore, will be the thickest and tend to slope downwards. As we move up the tree, the branches will become progressively thinner and the angle to the trunk will level out through the middle section, whilst the higher branches will reach outwards and upwards towards the sky.

Branch Taper

Once again, the growth of the branches will reflect the growth of the trunk and show good taper. As we move from the main branch into the side branches and twigs, there should be a nice even flow with good natural taper and movement that follows the general rhythm of the tree. Branches should divide into two at regular, short intervals, which will provide more twigs and greater ramification. If you leave lots of branches emanating from one point, then this can lead to swelling and the formation of a large unsightly 'knuckle', especially where the branches are pulling in opposite directions. It is, therefore, better to eliminate excess buds/shoots as soon as possible to prevent this

This Chishio maple, seen here in its glorious spring colour, shows branches in harmony with each other and the trunk.

Side shoots are removed to prevent wide knuckles developing. The two branches remaining have been pruned back to short internodes, where new shoots are emerging.

Appearance vs Health

Over the years I have found some bonsai enthusiasts to be critical of other enthusiasts who buy a good-quality specimen bonsai imported from Japan, especially when such trees are presented in a competitive exhibition. Some people call it cheating, whilst others appear to believe that everything should be grown from a seed or cutting. If serious collectors were not prepared to invest heavily in these trees, then most of us would never have the opportunity to see magnificent, well-ramified, specimen bonsai in the flesh and we would be restricted to pictures in books and magazines. Furthermore, being able to work on this material enables us to learn advanced ramification and maintenance techniques that can then be made available for bonsai enthusiasts in general. What people fail to appreciate is that whilst it takes a certain amount of skill and knowledge to create and build up a tree, it takes a different but equally important skill set to improve and keep a specimen bonsai looking impressive, whilst maintaining it in good health.

Your tree needs to grow foliage to put roots on in order to be strong and healthy. You control the growth on a specimen bonsai very strictly to maintain its shape and ramification but this could weaken the tree. Allow it to grow too much and you could lose your refined image: fine branches become too thick and have to be cut back. You really have to think about what you are doing and balance the growth correctly. If you are planning to exhibit a tree, then in the growing season leading up to the event you should concentrate all your efforts on appearance. Growth is monitored and pruned precisely for shape; watering and feeding are carefully controlled to restrict foliage size but maintain it in good health. Your aim is to have the tree at its peak just as the exhibition arrives and presentation is immaculate. In the growing season after the exhibition, you should concentrate your efforts on health and vigour. Watering and feeding return to normal and more growth is encouraged and allowed, but still controlled, so as not to spoil the refined branch structure built up over many years. This is an ongoing delicate balancing act that you have to learn to master once your bonsai reaches this specimen level.

Top Right: July 2013 and this old yamadori juniper from Japan has been allowed to grow strongly to build up vigour and good health.

Right: Exactly one year later and the tree is back under control and being refined back to its top level. I had this tree in my collection for more than thirteen years.

problem developing. The point at which buds emerge on a stem is called a node and the distance between these nodes is the internode. When we are building the ramification and refining our trees, it is desirable to have the internodes as short as possible to keep the tree compact and in scale. Left unchecked, long internodes will push the edge of the foliage canopy too far away from the trunk, so that the tree loses its shape and scale, branches become leggy, whilst inner shoots become weaker and die.

Method

Deciduous Trees

Maples continue to be one of the most popular subjects for deciduous bonsai trees and dominate the detailed advice given in this section. However, the basic principles and underlying techniques discussed here can be applied to most deciduous species of bonsai.

Maples: Example 1

A young maple, Tree 1, in April, after that first early flush of growth.

Too many branches emerging from the same point.

Offending branches are removed, leaving the main trunk with movement and taper.

A second maple, Tree 2, with the trunk splitting into three possible trunks.

A side trunk is removed but the low branch could be useful and is retained.

A single trunk but now with heavier low branches for age and character.

May and Tree 2 now resembles a dense bush.

Large leaves are removed, the top is controlled, lower branches are allowed to extend.

July and a well-angled shoot has emerged from one of the cut back trunks.

The long, low branch is thickening well and there is a good side-shoot to eventually cut back to.

Tree in July and potential secondary branches have extended in the upper area.

They are cut back to the tree's profile. Lower ones are left uncut.

Maples: Example 2

January 2019 – another maple lifted from the growing bed, now older and bigger.

April 2019 – repotted, pruned back to shape and now leafing out.

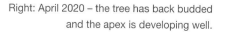

May 2019 – allowed to grow and recover with some control to the apex.

Right: April 2020 – the tree has back budded and the apex is developing well.

5

The growing tips of the apex are cut back as they emerge to control and refine.

Right: May 2020 – controlling the top has allowed lower branches to grow stronger.

6

7

Leaves are thinned out allowing light in the canopy. Secondary branches are allowed to grow to thicken.

8

June 2020 – more new growth stimulated especially in the stronger apex.

9

10

11

Top Left: The apex is brought under control and shoots to let grow or cut back are selected depending on thickness.

Above: July 2020 – the tree continues to grow well and shoots extend, but under my control.

Left: Once again a selection has been made, always keeping the stronger apex under control.

November 2019 – lower branches on this trident maple have been allowed to grow but are now pulling upwards.

March 2020 – wired and pulled down, the branches now give the image of an older more mature tree.

In the early stages of developing your tree, a regular pattern will emerge. Some branches will be allowed to extend to thicken or create secondary branches, whilst faster-growing, stronger areas, like the apex, will be kept under control by pinching out the growing tips as they open. As branches grow and become stronger, it is easy for them to get out of control and some wiring may be required to redefine the shape of the tree.

As the image of your tree improves and the main/secondary branches are in place, you will then be concentrating on creating more and more fine twigs by pinching most parts of the tree. To maintain vigour and good health, you may have to let some lower branches extend from time to time to promote more root growth. Done carefully this will also help you to continue to build

Right: August 2020 – some branches have been allowed to extend while the apex has been controlled and pinched back.

15

Branches are pruned back to the profile of the tree and the benefits of the wiring now become more obvious.

Have branches breaking into pairs all the way from the main branch to the outer twigs. Here the centre one is the obvious one to remove.

All twigs with long internodes need to be cut back.

Removing this thick section will improve the taper in the branch.

up the lower branches. Allowing the tree to flex its muscles in these lower branches can also help it accept and be more cooperative in holding back growth in the areas that you are trying to refine. If you let areas in the upper section of the tree extend too far, then they will become too thick, you will lose your ramification and they will have to be removed and regrown.

Just as your tree loses its leaves in the autumn is a good time to carry out pruning work on the current season's growth. You have between one and two weeks to carry out this work before the sap stops flowing and your tree will then bleed if cut. Try one branch and if this is alright, then you can continue. If it bleeds, then apply some sealant and you will have to postpone your pruning until spring when the sap is flowing again. It is better if you can carry out this refinement pruning in the autumn because it helps to stimulate the emergence of new buds over the winter. If you prune in spring, it tends to stimulate more the buds you already have. Adopt a methodical approach, working over the tree branch by branch. You are looking to remove

Large knuckles like this need to be reduced to two shoots or removed completely.

Prune just behind the bud in front and the next bud will extend the growth to the right.

Prune here and the branch will grow from the bud behind to the left. This is directional pruning.

branches that are crossing or growing inwards, and cut back any long internodes and twigs projecting too far beyond the canopy of the tree. Avoid leaving large knuckles where too many shoots are emerging from one point and, where possible, try to improve the taper in your branches.

Where a deciduous tree has buds that alternate along a branch, you can control the direction of the branch by pruning in front of the bud that is on the side where you want the branch to continue to grow. Don't prune too close to buds but leave at least a centimetre to dieback naturally. This will help to protect the bud and can be easily removed at a later date.

When you first style a tree or carry out the initial pruning, the instant change in the material can be quite dramatic. It is exciting, inspiring and will often reinvigorate your enthusiasm for the hobby. Refinement work is a slow process. You carry out basically the same routines year after year and often there seems little change in your tree. It can be a little disheartening but you have to persevere because one day the tree will surprise you. You will be going through the usual process and routines but then as you step back and take a look at your tree, suddenly it hits you. The tree has changed dramatically again but this time it has taken a few years to achieve the transformation. This is a never-ending process because whatever level your tree is at, there is always another higher level you can achieve, so just enjoy the journey. Take another look at the ongoing work with 'Big John', my trident maple in the Case Study at the end of Chapter 5.

Maples: Example 3 – Sango-Kaku Maple

November 2012 – the tree has been allowed to grow unchecked to provide us with a selection for our basic branch structure.

Selection made and cut back for a basic framework. The lower carved hollow is where the original trunk was cut off. The rest of the trunk was just a thin side branch.

February 2014 – lower branches are thickening nicely and the tree has had a wiring to improve the positioning of the branches.

November 2014 – side shoots have been allowed to grow to provide some secondary branches.

November 2016 – side shoots have been allowed to extend approximately 5cm and then stopped by pinching out the growing tip.

Now we are into our autumn pruning routine and the new growth has been selectively pruned, as we detailed earlier in this chapter.

November 2017 – the growing process has been repeated, but each year the ramification and density of twigs is improving.

Right: Even after another autumn pruning, the tree is beginning to show a nice winter image with a good underlying branch structure. Five years but the difference is dramatic!

Hedging Material as Bonsai

Species of shrubs and trees that are commonly used as hedging material in gardens often make excellent bonsai subjects. They are often quite tough, forgiving varieties that respond well to regular, hard pruning. Their leaves also tend to be on the small side, which makes it easier to create the image of a large tree in miniature. I discussed collecting material from the garden in Chapter 2 and old, established hedges are capable of yielding some excellent potential bonsai. The initial styling of this material will involve some branch selection and, possibly, the wiring of major branches. Once you have established the basic framework of the canopy around the trunk, it is possible to do a lot of the development work on this material using the clip and grow method. It almost becomes like topiary but, instead of carving out a chicken, you are trying to portray the image of a tree. Spaces will have to be incorporated into the design and, as the foliage becomes denser, you will have to go inside some of the branches to thin out shoots and to reduce congestion. Species to look out for include *Cotoneaster, Lonicera, Ligustrum* (privet), *Pyracantha, Berberis* and *Escallonia*.

Example 1: *Lonicera nitidia*

Above: April 2016 – a large *Lonicera* garden plant now established in a bread tray.

Top Right: An initial branch selection followed by basic wiring of the main branches.

Right: March 2017 – the tree grew back well after the pruning and has just been repotted.

Above: A view from the other side and another possible front for this tree.

Top Right: July 2020 – the tree has grown really well and once again resembles a bush.

Right: No wiring, just another pruning, but now you can see the image of the tree.

Example 2: Golden Privet

April 2017 – dug out of a hedge 2015, potted up and now with lots of new growth.

After the first branch selection, top branches short, lower ones left long.

Above: July 2017 – lower branches wired down and amazing new growth.

Middle Right: August 2017 – lower branches left alone but the apex area is cut back short.

Right: June 2018 – this material responds so well to being pruned and well fed.

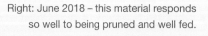

Once again the apex is cut back short while the lower branches thicken.

June 2019 – the apex is really developing well and now we can reduce the lower branches.

Amazing progress in just two years. Now we can build up foliage on the lower branches.

Coniferous Trees

With most conifers, the strength in the tree is in the tips of the foliage at the ends of the branches. The strong tips are responsible for drawing the sap along the branch, so that as the outer branches extend, they will draw inner branches to also grow and extend behind them. When you are developing these trees, you often have to let outer branches extend beyond the canopy and then these can be shortened once the inner shoots are strong enough to replace them. You have to transfer the vigour from the outer, stronger branches to the inner, weaker branches. When you are cleaning out needles/foliage and pruning back you will take more from stronger areas and leave weak areas untouched, so that you can balance the vigour in the tree and have it growing in equilibrium.

The objectives we had with the deciduous trees remain basically the same in trying to create a good, natural-looking, underlying structure, with tapering branches supporting foliage clouds of fine twigs and buds. Main branches and secondary side branches can be allowed to extend when you are trying to build up the basic structure and increase branch thickness. When the side branches are strong enough, they can be wired out in keeping with the overall design of the tree to create the profile upon which fine shoots can be grown to form the foliage cloud.

Junipers

It would appear that arguments continue to rage over whether you should use scissors or a pinching technique when dealing with the pruning of junipers. In my early bonsai years, the general consensus in books and articles was to pinch out the tips of the foliage to keep the clouds under control. I have already stated that the growing tip is the strongest point and the focus of the tree's energy. If you pinch out a large area of growing tips, you leave a disfiguring mass of weak, browning tips and if this is carried out extensively over the whole tree, then the tree will be considerably weakened and could even die. You have to be careful not to remove too much strong foliage from a juniper all at once. When you discuss this topic with anyone who has been taught by the Japanese, it becomes obvious that your pruning technique should mostly involve the use of scissors to selectively prune an individual shoot behind the tip but leaving other adjacent, small side-shoots to take its place.

There are two foliage types we generally encounter: one, like *Juniperus chinensis* has a fine, needle-type foliage, whilst the other, such as *Juniperus squamata meyerii*, has buds or scale-like foliage. As the juniper canopy becomes dense and bushy, it needs to be thinned out to allow more light and air to enter the canopy. This work would also be carried out prior to a wiring and styling of the tree. Inner, weak shoots are removed but the stronger, bright-green shoots at the tips are left untouched. Some poorly placed, crossing or overly long branches may also be removed in line with this work.

This thinning out process will encourage new buds to develop inside the canopy especially at branch junctions. New, bright, emerging, strong shoots should be left untouched during this cleaning out process. Only weak, old shoots should be removed.

During the growing season, the outer tips will start to extend. If the tree has been recently repotted, is weak or we just want to build up or extend the branches, then the tips can be allowed to extend unchecked in order to build up vigour. As we begin to refine a strong, healthy tree and maintain its good appearance, then we can prune back the extending shoots earlier when they are much shorter.

The tip can be removed or we can cut further back as long as there are strong side shoots to take its place.

Compare the dull weak inner shoot with the strong swollen bright green tips of the outer shoots.

These new emerging inner shoots will promote vigour in the tree and can ultimately be used to replace adjacent overly long branches.

Shoots left unchecked to thicken/extend branches and generally make the tree stronger.

To maintain the profile of a strong healthy tree, once shoots have extended beyond the profile they can be cut back to the canopy outline when they are much shorter.

Example 1: *Juniperus squamata meyerii*

September 2016 – the tree is growing strong but is in danger of losing its shape and reverting back to being a bush.

Some branches are removed and the inner areas are generally cleaned out so the tree is ready for wiring.

Upward-growing shoots can be pinched back to form the outline of a shallow cloud. Outward-growing tips can extend to maintain vigour.

Right: September 2018 – foliage areas are beginning to fill out and some more thinning out is required.

The tree wired and styled with side branches spread out to form the base of the foliage clouds.

The pattern of foliage clouds making up the canopy are now beginning to emerge. Any downward-pointing shoots below branches are removed.

September 2019 – the tree stands without any wire and spaces within the canopy are more clearly defined.

8

August 2020 – the foliage is becoming much tighter as the image matures.
The overall canopy is narrowing to harmonize with the tall slender trunk.

Pines

Japanese black pines (*Pinus thunbergii*) and Japanese red pines (*Pinus densiflora*) are capable of two flushes of growth each year, whereas Scots pines (*Pinus sylvestris*), mugo pines (*Pinus mugo*) and Japanese white pines (*Pinus parviflora*) only have one flush of growth. This will influence how we treat the two types of tree. With strong, black and red pines, we can cut away the current season's candle growth, as soon as the candle has produced needles. This will usually be between the end of May and July, depending on your climate. Aim to do this work as early as possible, so that you have more of the growing season left to produce the second crop of candles. This technique is used to produce shoots with shorter internodes and smaller needles, so it is more of a refinement technique. We can also help to balance the vigour in the tree, if necessary, by leaving any weak candles alone, cutting the medium-strength candles first and the stronger candles around two weeks later. If you are still developing branches or trying to encourage back-budding, then it is better to let branches and shoots extend more in the way we treat single-flush pines.

With single-flush pines, I prefer to let them have the season's growth and then clean out needles and select buds/shoots as we go into autumn. This will keep the trees growing strongly and encourage more back-budding. Overly long shoots can be pruned back to strong, inner shoots and multiple buds can be pruned back to two well-placed shoots. Any buds growing downwards underneath the branches are removed. The pinching back of candles early in the season is more a grooming technique that can be carried out on established bonsai that already have a good branch structure and well-defined foliage clouds. As candles extend and reach the edge of the tree's profile, the tip can be pinched out with fingers, but leave a few pairs of needles to develop further. Most bonsai enthusiasts tend to find themselves working on pine material that still needs more branch/twig development.

May 2020 – a white pine. Some strong shoots need to be cut back. The pink flowers will fall away by themselves.

The strong shoots have been reduced and the older needles cleaned out to let more light and air in.

If you have a long branch with no inner buds, you may just have to let the candle develop, open out and harden-off, then cut it back leaving a few pairs of needles. This will usually be around mid-summer: mid-May to mid-July in the UK. This can create some back-budding, especially if the tree is strong and well fertilized.

We can use the distribution of needles to balance the vigour in the tree. If you are starting with a project in spring, look over the strong branches, which are usually near the apex, and compare them with the weaker, lower branches. On the denser, stronger branches, reduce the needles to say ten or twelve pairs and leave the lighter, thinner branches untouched. Aim to remove needles that are hanging below branches, and also remove needles from around bud and small-branch joints to visually sepa-rate them. This work can be repeated in the autumn after a full season's growth. Leave some of the old needles, as well as the new needles, to help the tree overcome any adverse conditions.

Look closely for the new buds. More light and excess vigour pushed back into the tree will help these develop.

Example 1: Scots Pine Twin Trunk

December 2015 – a garden centre Scots pine.

January 2016 – after its first wiring and styling. When it is repotted the planting angle will be changed as shown.

October 2017 – needles have been cleaned out and the tree is beginning to look more like a bonsai than a bush.

December 2020 – after another wiring the denser foliage clouds and spaces are becoming more clearly defined.

Example 2: Scots Pine Semi-Cascade

Above: March 2013 – another garden centre Scots pine.

Top Right: After examining the trunk and branches we decided to alter the planting angle and as you can see the initial pruning was quite drastic!

Right: October 2017 – seasonal growth and some light summer pruning have paved the way for an autumn wiring enabling us to redefine the foliage clouds and spaces.

December 2018 – after some cleaning out of needles the structure of the tree is now clearly visible again and inner buds will receive adequate light and air.

November 2019 – now rewired and reshaped the tree has broader denser branches creating a more mature image.

September 2020 – a repotting has helped contain the vigour and reduce the needle size but not stopped the foliage clouds achieving greater density.

Now we can take out some of the stronger outer shoots leaving shorter inner shoots behind to take over. Vigour is maintained and density increased.

Seven years working on this tree might seem like a long time but in bonsai terms this is relatively short. More important is that you can see the transformation.

Cedars

Once again, you have to let branches grow, so that when they are strong enough, they can then be wired to form the basis of the foliage clouds. Once you have the foliage clouds established, you can pinch out the tips of upward-growing shoots in line with the branch profile. Outward-growing tips can be allowed to extend to build up the branch and maintain vigour. If the branch is thick enough, you can prune back the new growth to the tree's outline after it has extended two to three inches. Leave the shoots to grow if the branch is weak or you need more thickness. You can also use this technique to balance the vigour in the tree between any weaker, lower branches and the stronger apex.

Example 1: *Cedar libani*

December 2016 – a large cedar brought to a workshop for advice on the initial styling.

A selection of branches was made and all the unwanted ones were pruned away leaving a basic triangular shape.

3 The tree seen from the other side. The tree was strong and the growing tips of the selected branches were left to grow.

Right: June 2018 – the tree has been kept under some control. The overall shape of the canopy is clearly visible and more dense.

4

5 The overall shape of the canopy is clearly visible and more dense. November 2019 – the tree is wired and the foliage clouds and spaces are now much more clearly defined.

6 August 2020 – now we are already seeing greater density. Outward-growing tips are unpruned, whilst upward-growing shoots are controlled.

Larch

Often referred to as the deciduous conifer because its needle-like foliage classifies it with other similar conifers but it sheds all its foliage over the winter months. The bark on larch is quite thick and swells quickly, so keeping the dominant apex under control becomes even more important, otherwise you will lose any ramification that you have built up and will have to regrow overly heavy branches. As with the other conifers that we have discussed, lower branches can be allowed to extend to thicken and maintain vigour. The tree can be allowed to leaf out and put on its vivid green coat but then, as shoots begin to extend out of the green florets, they can be pinched back in early summer in line with the foliage profile. Shoots on the exterior of the cloud, growing horizontally outwards, can be allowed to extend slightly. Once the tree has shed its foliage in the autumn, the tree's structure will be clearly visible and it can be pruned back to shape, as required. Where possible, you will be looking to replace thick, outer branches with thinner, inner branches to improve taper and to build up your ramification. Once your tree starts to mature and has good ramification, you will find that you will be pruning the new growth back to leave only one or two buds. Winter is also the time to wire and style larch while the branches are bare. I would normally wire first and then prune back to shape, when the overall profile is more clearly visible. If the tree is growing strongly, you will have to keep a close eye on the wiring in the following summer because it will soon start biting in as the bark swells. I would also normally repot larch quite early in the spring because you should never disturb their roots when they are showing green foliage, as they are prone to completely collapsing.

Example 1: Young Nursery Material

A young larch clump of seedlings pictured here at the very end of May.

The growing tip is cleanly removed to control the stronger apex and prevent further shoot extension.

Example 2: Older Shohin-Size Larch

1

A larch rock combination in November after the season's growth has been initially shortened.

2

Thicker, outer branches can be cut back to inner, thinner branches to improve taper.

3

This long branch can be reduced and long internodes on the new growth cut back to keep the tree compact.

4

The tree is now much more compact, branches are in scale with the trunk and we can continue with more refinement.

Taxus (Yew)

You will probably encounter several varieties of the European yew (*Taxus baccata*) and also the Japanese yew (*Taxus cuspidata*). As discussed in previous chapters, and also in the earlier section on conifers, you have to let your trees grow and extend, especially in the earlier years of training. Yews are no exception to the rule and this applies when we are thickening up the basic branch structure and also building up the secondary ramification. Strong, extended growth of the main branch and side shoots will help the thickening process. When we start to build up the side branches and ramification, we can allow some extension of shoots until we are in a position to prune back to new, shorter growth nearer the main branch and trunk. Promoting growth and vigour will create more back-bud-

ding and finer shoots, which we can then use to build up the foliage clouds. When wiring the tree to create the initial shape and subsequently to form the outline of the foliage pads, try to avoid any period when you see that new buds are breaking in order to avoid damaging them. I normally look over the yews in early summer, after the first flush of strong growth, to see if I can prune any long shoots back to shorter side shoots. This growth inside will then have the rest of the season to develop and extend. As the foliage clouds become denser and more refined, I can pinch out the growing tips as they emerge in spring, especially with *Taxus cuspidata*. Once again, we can use the pinching and pruning techniques to correct any imbalance in the tree by allowing weaker areas to grow unchecked, whilst controlling any stronger-growing sections.

Example 1: Twin-Trunk Hedging Yew

Above: July 2018 – originally dug out of a garden hedge, this golden yew is becoming well established as a bonsai and has grown well the previous season.

Top Right: Now we can select branches in the best position/angle and prune back those that are overly long to redefine the shape of the two trees.

Right: October 2020 – the tree has been allowed to grow again with just moderate but similar intervention. Already the image is much denser and more mature looking.

Example 2: Semi-Cascade Garden Tree

January 2016 – this was originally a tall garden tree that we drastically reduced to one branch and then tilted over. Here the basic outline is established.

August 2017 – after eighteen months of allowing growth and then pruning back, the branches are filling out and we can make the tree much more compact.

December 2018 – the lower branches have been removed completely and pruning of the new shoots has produced dense foliage clouds, which can now be pinched.

Example 3: *Taxus cuspidata*

Left: March 2020 – this tree was used as an example of driftwood style bonsai in Chapter 3 and pictured here in spring, the extensive back-budding is clearly visible.

Left: April 2020 – the upper foliage clouds and crown are established and dense, so we can pinch this new growth. The weaker lower branches are left to grow and extend.

As the new shoot opens it is gently grasped between the finger and thumb and carefully removed. This will keep twigs fine, increase density and maintain the profile.

Satsuki Azaleas

There are just so many varieties of this popular, spectacular, flowering bonsai producing different colours and variations, often on the same tree. Its natural tree-like qualities in the spreading nebari, trunk/branches and small leaves, already make it an excellent bonsai subject; the flowers are a fantastic bonus.

Most of the work we do on these trees is immediately after flowering and this can include repotting. Depending on the weather and the variety, in my climate the trees are capable of flowering from around mid-May to late-July. I try to have all the pruning work completed before the end of August, as the trees

For a few months each year the Satsuki azalea bonsai is totally transformed.

Removing just the petals leaves the base of the flower intact.

This furry little stump you have left will produce a seed pod.

Cleanly pinch the stem supporting the flower from below.

start to form next year's flower buds quite early and if you leave the pruning too late, then you could be removing next year's flowers. When I have exhibited azaleas in flower, if I wanted to speed up the flowering process, then I would keep the tree on the dry side and in a sunny spot. If I wanted to slow the flowering down, then I would keep the soil more moist and place it in a cool, sheltered, shady position. As soon as a flower fades or is past its best, it needs to be removed, but you need to remove the whole stem at its base and not just the flower petals. If you leave the stem and flower stalk it will produce seed pods, which are then using up the tree's energy.

When it comes to pruning azaleas you have to remember that in their wild, natural state they are a low-growing, wide-spreading bush. They are, therefore, very strong in the lower branches growing outwards and weak in the branches that form the apex. From reading this book you will already have realized that this contradicts how we have treated most other trees that tend to be almost always apical dominant. This means we can prune strongly the outward-growing, lower branches but always treat the apex with respect and just prune lightly, the minimum amount required to maintain its shape. By the time the last flowers are removed, the tree will already be producing new shoots and is ready for pruning. The work detailed here is carried out on a young, strong, vigorous tree. If your tree is weak, then leave it to recover and regain strength first. Each branch is considered, and its position and what we want to achieve will determine which of the pruning options is selected.

7 August 2020 – dead flowers can be removed and branches can be considered for pruning.

Satsuki Azaleas (cont'd)

In strong trees, multiple shoots will emerge from behind the dead flower bud.

Just prune back to the best-placed two shoots and leave them to extend if you want more branch development.

Normal pruning, allowing some extension of the canopy, is pruning back to two shoots and two leaves.

Right: If we want to contain the tree and take it back to where we started the season, then prune back to where the shoots emerge.

Far right: If the tree has extended too far, then we can just cut back into the old wood to the length we require.

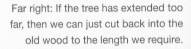

Left: The tree after pruning, lightly at the top and selective lower down, with shoots left long to build up these branches.

January 2021 – an abundance of back-budding after carrying out the pruning work.

CHAPTER 9

BONSAI AESTHETICS

Introduction

Bonsai are generally categorized with plants and garden-ing, after all it is a living tree or shrub. However, if it were left to grow naturally, it would be just another plant and would lack the charm, charisma and fascination associated with bonsai. It is the style and arrangement of its parts, the control that we exert over the tree that transforms it from being a naturally growing organism into a living work of art. Sadly, this is not always appreciated as much as it should be by the artistic fraternity. Dictionary definitions of 'aesthet-ics' include 'a set of principles concerned with the nature and appreciation of beauty' and 'a branch of philosophy that deals with questions of beauty and artistic taste'. If you stand in awe before a mature bonsai in an exhibition and are blown away by its appearance, this is no accident. The tree's basic design must be good, the branch structure or elements within the design are working well and the exe-cution of the twigs and foliage clouds is immaculate. If you look at a bonsai and feel uncomfortable with its appear-ance then something in its design or execution is wrong and not working. I accept that beauty is in the eye of the beholder and what appeals to one person may not appeal to another. However, if I can try to help you to appreciate the philosophy and principles behind the aesthetics, then hopefully this will help you to create better-looking bonsai that will not only be more satisfying to you, but will also be communicated to anyone you invite to view them.

Sources of Inspiration

Nature

When contemplating trying to create a miniature tree, it is obvious that our primary source of inspiration will be trees that we have seen in nature. You have been surrounded by trees for most of your life but probably took them for granted and never studied or appreciated them. As your interest in bonsai grows, you will start to see trees in a whole new light. You will appreciate their magnificence and beauty, you will find fault in their branch structure and

Below: An old tree in the grounds of Nostell Priory with massive low branches reaching to become almost second trunks. These would be removed by the ardent bonsai enthusiast.

be only too happy to prune off any wayward branches; in essence, you will start to understand trees.

With so much haphazard, dense growth over many years, natural trees can be very complicated, so when you try to replicate this in your bonsai, it is a much more simplified version. Notice how the heaviest and oldest branches are the lowest, how they sag with age, how younger branches reach outwards for more light, how trunks and branches taper. The harshness of the local climate may seriously affect a tree, causing damage to its trunk or branches and forcing it to grow in one direction. Such strong, vivid, individual characteristics can linger in the memory and often leads to the creation of a very dramatic bonsai at some point in the future.

Japan

Images of amazing Japanese bonsai are perhaps something that draws most of us into this hobby in the first place. When I see pictures of rows of old bonsai in a

This white pine is a classic Japanese bonsai image with its huge broad canopy.

Japanese nursery it still blows me away even now. They are magnificent and we spend most of our bonsai lives trying to impose this image on our own trees, but rarely do you see a tree like this when you're out walking. It's almost like the Japanese are trying to create the perfect tree and show Mother Nature 'this is how trees should be'.

In my early bonsai years, with translated articles it became very obvious that the Japanese approach was very regimental and calculated with a strict and somewhat repetitive arrangement of branches. The placement of branches around the trunk was carefully measured and set out in detail. It caused me much frustration as I struggled to impose this strict regime on my basic material that had somewhat inadequate branches and none of them seemingly in the right place. I now take great pleasure in recreating a Japanese image in my work but one that is more relaxed, following the basic principles, but working with the branches I have available and growing new branches where it is viable to do so. One of my mentors and a good friend, Dan Barton, used to say, 'If we can't create a miniature tree let's create a bonsai'. Differentiating between these two sources and having a sound idea of what you are actually trying to create can be invaluable in achieving the right result.

The Living Sculpture

Trees in this group are very conceptual in form, often displaying a large amount of deadwood and with just a small amount of foliage sufficient to keep the tree alive. Their shape and form can be quite dynamic, a product of the artist's imagination and appreciated, literally, as a living sculpture, rather than a tree we have seen growing naturally. We are using a tree to create an object of beauty. However, that is not to say that these trees don't exist in nature. Junipers and pines growing in extreme weather conditions and at high altitudes can exhibit the most amazing, intricate deadwood and trunk shapes, as they continuously battle to survive.

Styling Considerations

The basic design considerations outlined in Chapter 3 still hold good but now we need to take the thought process a little further. When we start with a piece of raw material, we can recall images of natural trees or bonsai as a source of reference and then manipulate the branches to depict an image broadly resembling this tree. The same tree or raw material will be interpreted differently by different artists,

A tree in Nevada literally living on the edge where survival is a constant battle with nature.

depending on their experience and ability. A photograph or painting of a tree is just one point in time and will reflect the tree's natural appearance with its complicated array of branches. Our artistic creation as a bonsai is alive and needs to be simplified because we have to consider the tree's health and its future development, it needs a plan for the rest of its life to maintain and develop its appearance.

Right: A young oak tree with similar relatively thin branches making an upward-pointing, fan-like silhouette. Such trees often have a much narrower canopy.

Mature trees with broad dense canopies characterized by a wide domed crown.

Age and Character

The age of the tree that you are trying to replicate can have a profound effect on the character of the trunk and the arrangement of branches. The character of the trunk and branches in your raw material may dictate the category of tree you can create.

The more you can match the characteristics of your bonsai with recollections of trees you have seen growing in nature, the more convincing your illusion of a miniature tree will be.

An older tree with sparser foliage clouds and a trunk scarred with dead stumps that were once mighty branches.

In really old and ancient trees, the rotting-down of the trunk escalates and often only a few, low, side-branches remain to keep the tree alive.

Above: This Korean hornbeam has an old-looking trunk but the upper canopy is tall, pointed and youthful.

Top Right: If we reduce the canopy, making it wider and more rounded, it will be more in keeping with the trunk.

Right: Immediately this bonsai looks more comfortable and suggests the image of an older, more mature tree.

Is Your Tree Tall or Short?

When styling your tree, the branches you select, wire and grow should relate to the trunk they are growing from. Tall conifers, with a relatively thin trunk having little taper, will have short branches and foliage close to the trunk, reminiscent of forest trees growing close together.

At the other extreme, once-massive trees now rotting down, or bonsai having short, powerful, stocky trunks, will have heavy branches and a foliage canopy that is often as wide as it is tall.

This mighty sequoia tree was growing in the grounds of a hotel.

A very comparable natural-looking image where *Juniperus chinensis* 'Blaauws' have been convincingly fixed to a dead *Juniperus rigida* stump.

Example: *Juniperus squamata meyerii*

Right: The straight, upper trunk on this juniper was cut back and lower branches were allowed to grow unchecked.

Far Right: You can see here the stub where it was cut back as it lacked interest and taper.

The lower section has much more potential and the long side-branches were finally cut back.

Left: The deadwood is created and extended, leaving separate veins to feed the two remaining branches.

Right: The branches are cleaned out and wired ready for styling. The live veins and deadwood interact well.

Now we have a small, powerful tree with a foliage canopy in keeping with the tree's stocky bonsai image.

This *Potentilla* has been recently repotted at a new angle to improve the root base but the branches are now disturbing – the right ones are pointing upwards and the left ones downwards.

Digitally adjusted, the pot is now at a precarious angle but the branches are much better returned to the horizontal. The lower left-hand branch was removed as it was too thin, opposite the main branch on the right and would now have been growing into the branch above.

Balance and Stability

The bonsai tree must be well balanced and stable; it must not look like it is falling out of the pot. When this is achieved, the tree will be pleasing and comfortable on the eye. The pointed apex in the Korean hornbeam is leading you upwards out of the design, whereas the rounded apex outlined by the hand and reduced in the third picture is gently lowering you down the tree towards the ground. The ground or soil surface of the pot, the horizontal, is an important baseline and how the branches or foliage clouds relate to this baseline will affect the balance and stability of the tree's appearance. If you imagine a line running through the centre of each branch or cloud, then this should be parallel to the horizontal baseline. This stabilizing effect not only ties each branch to the base, but also links each branch to one another, creating a calm sense of balance over the whole tree.

This old cedar in Bretton Sculpture Park is making an excellent effort to create separate well-balanced foliage clouds.

Rhythm and Harmony

There is a certain rhythm running through your tree that may become more obvious with deciduous trees when the underlying structure is clearly visible. In nature, the trunk and branches grow in the same conditions and are subject to the same extremes of nature. In good, calm

With this maple, the lower branch is growing upwards, whilst the upper branches, which should be angled, are horizontal. The branches are out of sync with one another and the base.

There is a better and more natural rhythm with this tree as branches become thinner and more angled as they progress up the trunk, culminating in a nice, rounded apex.

Right: The best Chinese elm I ever had, with well-balanced foliage clouds in harmony with each other, a nice natural rhythm and well-rounded, mature crown.

conditions, if a trunk is able to grow perfectly straight, then the branches will also be relatively straight, other than having to reach out for light. In an extreme location, when a tree is being tossed about by winds and storms, the trunk may exhibit many twists and turns and this would also be reflected in the way the branches grow too. If all your branches are growing out at a certain downward angle and then suddenly one branch is growing upwards totally against the rhythm of the rest, then this will create discord and stand out dramatically. Ideally, the tree should be in perfect harmony, stable and well balanced, and the branches in sync with one another, both in terms of shape and density/vigour. All the branches and foliage clouds should demonstrate the same state of good health and strength.

This yamadori larch is pictured here in spring. The gentle curves in the trunk are picked up in the branches, creating a nice, relaxed style, with even growth and no wiring.

I exhibited this *Juniperus chinensis ittogawa* twice at the Ginkgo Awards in Belgium. Despite its gentle, downward slope, the healthy foliage clouds are in balance with the horizontal and each other.

Movement, Energy and Space

Spaces define and give a crisp edge to the foliage clouds, whilst the foliage clouds surround, frame and capture the space. The relationship between these two elements can have a dramatic effect on the appearance of the tree and determine whether its design is a success or a failure. Negative spaces can affect the balance of the tree, highlighting the relationship between individual branches and also create a sense of instability between the tree and the pot. The underside of the branches should always be kept clean by removing any downward-growing twigs or foliage. In nature, these would be weak and eventually die due to a lack of light or be grazed on by animals.

The bonsai itself may be a static object but there are directional forces within the composition that draw the viewer through the tree. Initially, the viewer may be attracted to a specific feature or the apex of the tree, and then be drawn through the design by a space or long, low branch. In a forest planting, for example, the tallest tree may be the initial attraction and then the viewer can be drawn to the left or right by smaller outward-leaning trees or a larger space within the pot. This invisible energy must be controlled and directed accordingly, otherwise it can draw the viewer out of the composition and result in an unsatisfactory feeling about the tree.

Notice how both bottom branches are parallel to the soil surface and how the yew burr stand mirrors the pot. The negative spaces bring perfect harmony and drama to this composition. To the right, the slope on the pot and stand are parallel to the low visible trunk.

An excellent twin-trunk juniper from a Newstead exhibition, but that heavy low branch on the left is pulling the viewer in the wrong direction.

The low branch removed digitally and now the strong movement is correctly towards the scroll and accent plant, making the display cohesive and comfortable on the eye.

Juniper 'Grey Owl' and even something like a jin sticking out of the canopy can distract the viewer and lead you out of the composition, here pulling us to the left.

The jin digitally removed and the tree looks much more comfortable, as we are led from the powerful base through the canopy to the right.

Deadwood in Bonsai

Why Do We Introduce Deadwood Into Our Bonsai?

Deadwood on trees occurs naturally in the wild, especially on trees growing in high, mountainous regions or extreme and exposed locations. Branches and connected sections of trunk can suffer dieback as a result of disease, drought or simply old age. Trees can be damaged by animals and human beings. In creating our miniature representation of a tree it, therefore, appears to be a reasonable logical step that deadwood could also be included.

As previously stated, bonsai is an illusion – we are trying to create in miniature the image of a mature tree. In most cases, the material we are using to create this image is relatively young. By introducing deadwood into the design, we can make our finished image appear to be much older and more convincing, as though it has stood the test of time and suffered some hardship.

In the process of initially styling our bonsai and carrying out further development, we often have to prune away a lot of branches, which can leave too many unsightly pruning scars. Sometimes this can make the tree look artificial or manmade. By introducing some deadwood, and possibly linking or camouflaging some of these scars, we can make our creation appear more natural. This can be

Above: An old hawthorn showing a natural shari and amazing detail in the deadwood created by Mother Nature.

1

The original straight section of trunk has been pruned back to a thick branch, but there is a danger of inverse taper being created.

2

The introduction of a shari accentuates the movement in the trunk and creates an illusion of taper with the live vein now twisting underneath.

3

The tree wired and shaped with the taller, narrow image more aesthetically pleasing and the pruned stump now a deadwood feature.

particularly useful where we have cut back a heavy section of trunk to improve taper and alter the trunk line. Instead of leaving a large, ugly pruning scar, the trunk can be hollowed-out and become an important feature.

Deadwood can also be used to help us overcome design faults. Sometimes the material we are working on may have inverse taper in the trunk; basically, unlike a natural tree, the base of the trunk actually gets thinner rather than fatter. By carefully manipulating a line of deadwood into the trunk we can create an illusion of taper to rectify this problem. When a branch dies, rather than cut it off we can turn it into deadwood if it is advantageous to maintain the outline of the tree's profile.

The Basic Forms of Deadwood We Use

Jin

When we strip the bark off a branch or pruned stub it is referred to by the Japanese term a jin. This is much easier to do whilst the branch is still soft and sappy. Score around the base of the branch with your branch-cutter and then, after squeezing the bark with jin pliers, it is easy to strip off. Cut and tear the branch back to create grain and texture to make it look more natural.

The rhythm in the tree we discussed earlier applies to dead branches as well as to live ones. The dead branch will have grown in the same way as the live ones, so if they

Tools of 'Torture'

There are some people who think that bonsai is cruel, so if these people were to watch us creating deadwood, then in their eyes it would be a resounding victory for the prosecution! When it comes to creating deadwood there is simply no one better than Mother Nature. The detail, texture and character on old, natural, deadwood are just amazing and this is what you are trying to replicate. Using hand tools, such as your various pruning shears, jin pliers for tearing and an array of chisels, can produce very impressive results but can take a relatively long time too. Just like your work on the live foliage, deadwood can be worked and refined over the life of the tree, helped and improved by natural weathering.

When large areas of hardwood have to be removed, then often you have no alternative but to resort to power tools. Heavy-duty die grinders with the right bits can cut through the hardest wood like butter, whilst smaller power tools, such as a Dremel, can be used for refinement work. Unfortunately, most of the bits that accompany your newly purchased power tool are not really suitable for bonsai and more appropriate cutting bits can be acquired from specialist suppliers. As you would expect, all power tools have to be treated with respect. A bit rotating at 35,000 revolutions a minute can damage you and your trees. Beware of the tool kicking back as you grind through wood and slipping on to/removing foliage and branches that you desperately need. Practise on a piece of old driftwood from the beach and get a good feel for your tool before you attack your precious bonsai. Creating good, natural-looking deadwood will take time to master and it is something you really do need to practise. Try to avoid leaving marks where the power tool has been, as it makes it obvious the deadwood was manmade.

An angled carving chisel, jin pliers, a grafting knife and a chef's torch. Just some of the tools involved in the creation of deadwood.

A massive jin and natural shari on a huge old tree at Burghley House.

Use jin pliers to tear back the wood to create character and texture.

have all been wired down, then the dead branch should be wired down too. While the stripped branch is still sappy it can also be bent into place by gently applying heat using a chef's blowtorch. There is a different technique if the dead branch has already dried out. Wrap some damp kitchen towel around the area on the branch to be bent and then cover this with kitchen foil. This can then be heated with the blowtorch and gently bent into place using your jin pliers. Hold it in its final position, strip off the kitchen foil and then gently apply more heat to the exposed kitchen towel to dry it out. This should then hold the jin in place, but you can support it with a guy wire for a couple of weeks, if necessary, to stop it springing back to the original position. If you create a jin, you can shorten it, adjust it and if it still doesn't contribute to the overall design of the tree, then you can remove it completely. If you immediately cut an unwanted branch off completely, you have lost the option of deadwood and any improvement it could bring to the tree's image.

Shari

If a strip of bark is removed from a section of the trunk, then this is referred to as a shari. In nature, when a substantial branch or major root dies, the vein of bark linking the two can dieback on the trunk creating a natural shari. Driftwood-style bonsai are created when the predominant feature of the tree is deadwood and sometimes there may just be a single, narrow, live vein keeping the foliage alive.

Gently score the area of bark you wish to remove and then peel it back, ensuring that it follows the designated lines. Where possible, I try to gently peel the bark back and let the tree tell me where it wants to go, following a natural line; but I still have to guide it around the edges to control the movement. This works really well with junipers and yews, where often the veins will twist around the trunk. Be careful not to completely ring bark the whole tree when you effectively cut off the supply lines between the roots and the foliage. Don't try to do too much all at once. Suggest a line to the tree with a very narrow shari that can be gradually widened in subsequent years. The bark on larch is so thick and swells so quickly that a shari can be closed up during a single growing season and have to be remade. A shari can link jins together, create a sense of drama and totally alter the appearance of a tree.

Uro's and Hollow Trunks

Here the damage to the tree is internal rather than external and the small holes we often see are referred to as an uro. Water and the weather have probably invaded the tree and over time caused the heartwood to simply rot away. Old branch scars have now become holes and deep hollows, which can become home to birds and squirrels. Sometimes the inside of the trunk is totally hollow, a feature often found on really old and ancient trees.

This can look a really precarious situation and yet the tree appears to be thriving. In bonsai, this can be used to overcome the problem of massive pruning scars, especially when we are reducing a large tree or shrub dug from the ground. A visual problem can suddenly become the main feature of the tree, with branches and foliage manipulated to surround and show off the hollow trunk. Soft tissue can be removed using a small hand-chisel, but harder and larger volumes of wood will require the use of power tools.

This *Juniperus chinensis* has become a living sculpture, with narrow, live veins twisting round a trunk that is now predominantly deadwood.

This tree is relatively young and yet the centre of the trunk is hollow.

Treatment of Deadwood

Once we have created our deadwood, allow it to dry out and then it can be treated with jin fluid, which is lime sulphur. This will bleach the wood white and also help to preserve it. With trees like junipers and yews it is the contrast between the stark white of the deadwood, the bright green foliage and the rich, reddish-brown tints of the bark that produces such amazing images. With pines and deciduous trees, a greyer, more subdued finish to the deadwood produces a more natural and convincing effect. I have used artist's white and black poster paints added to the lime sulphur to create the desired effect but I know some people have used tea, coffee and ink to achieve the same result. It's a case of experimenting and keeping a record of the mix you use and how it affects the colour of the deadwood.

Just like preparing for an exhibition, we wash and clean the deadwood first. Before you apply the lime sulphur, wet the deadwood again because when you then apply it the moisture helps the wood absorb it and it is less likely to run on to the bark. I remember first being told this in a conversation with my friend Hotsumi Terrakawa. I was intrigued and asked if this was a tradition passed down by bonsai masters in Japan. The dream was shattered when Hotsumi picked up the bottle, pointed and promptly translated from Japanese into English something that basically said 'apply wet'. Don't put too much on otherwise it can dry bright yellow rather than white and it is more likely to run on to the bark and stain it. It does have a strong, unpleasant smell, so be warned if you are planning on doing this work in the kitchen! The best results are obtained in high humidity, but if you apply it in hot sunshine, it can dry too quickly and again take on a yellow tint. Mist spray with water if this is a problem to slow the drying process down. Apart from exhibitions, you can carry out this work annually to protect the deadwood and retain its colour.

A *Taxus cuspidata* (Japanese yew) with bark and deadwood ready for cleaning prior to wiring and styling.

The live veins will often swell and be created naturally, leaving us with the task of tidying up the dead areas in between.

The contrast between the bleached deadwood, cleaned bark and green foliage produces a dramatic image.

Choosing the Right Pot

I suppose choosing a bonsai pot for your tree can be likened to buying a pair of shoes but you don't get to try it on! You buy a pot at a bonsai show absolutely certain it will be a perfect fit for your tree only to find that when you get home it is unbelievably too big or too small. You do need some accurate measurements with you because it's surprising how easy it is to get it wrong. I suppose this is why my classes are so busy in the repotting season. At least when they get their tree out of the pot we have a few hundred to choose from so they know there is a good chance one will be a near perfect fit or a reasonable compromise. There are many excellent bonsai potters in Europe, each with their own distinctive style who can make you a pot specifically designed for your favourite tree.

Any pot you buy must have adequate drainage holes and if there are also smaller holes to thread the tie wires through, this can make the repotting task much easier. Most of the pots you will encounter will be frost-proof, but ask the question if you are not sure. Many of the pots that commercial indoor bonsai trees arrive in from China are a lighter coloured clay and are not frost-proof.

This *Juniperus procumbens* had just arrived from Japan in a pot that looked unbelievably too small.

Size and Shape

The Japanese would seem to under-pot their trees, often leaving you to wonder how such a large, full tree survives in such a small pot. Perhaps the high humidity they experience does take some pressure off the roots, coupled with a rigorous and strict watering regime. In the West, we tend to over-pot our trees, often based on the principle that the more soil there is around the roots, the easier the tree will be to look after. Certainly, if you have trees in full leaf in a very shallow pot on a hot summer's day, it does put you under more pressure to get the watering right. Larger pots are better for trees in training where we are trying to promote strong, vigorous growth. Once the tree has a more finished image and we are in the refinement stage, then aesthetic considerations can be taken into account.

Some trees actually prefer a specific type of pot. Maples do better in a shallower pot, which tends to hold more water in relative percentage terms, whilst encouraging outward horizontal root growth, which will improve the nebari. Pines don't like their feet standing in water and as the surface area of the soil dries more quickly, their roots are happiest in that middle soil area, so they prefer a deeper pot. Azaleas also prefer a deeper pot as their roots don't like heavy, wet soil, but they need to be able to access adequate water to support a canopy full of flowers.

This pot was made by John Pitt, specifically for my privet bonsai, with a subtle crackle glaze complementing the colour of the bark and making the pot appear much older.

My black pine had recently been repotted into this deep genuine Tokonama unglazed pot.

A Deshojo maple forest just coming into leaf in a shallow pot that is very much an understatement to this landscape composition.

Aesthetically, a powerful, short, heavy trunk will look better in a chunky, muscular, rectangular pot, whilst a taller landscape-type tree will look better in a shallower pot, which will enhance that feeling of space. Forest plantings look good in very shallow pots or on an irregular-shaped slab. When using shallow pots, it may be advisable to mound the soil up to sustain the tree's good health. As a guide, the depth of the pot should be similar to the diameter of the trunk at soil level. The length of the pot can be approximately two-thirds the height of the tree or relate to the spread of the foliage canopy, depending on style.

If the trunk is very straight and formal, then it may be better suited to the sharp lines of a rectangular, formal pot, whereas if the trunk is lighter and curving, an oval shape or pot with a soft corner might be more appropriate. Literati-style trees, which are light and with a lot of trunk movement, often look good in round pots curving inwards for a sense of greater stability. Sometimes the pot can echo a feature in the tree, which helps tie the two together. A curve on the outside of the pot might mirror a curve in the trunk above or an indented soft corner might match a connection in the tree between shari and live vein.

Right: A literati-style juniper with an inward curving pot that relates to the curves in the trunk whilst promoting a sense of greater stability.

A blue shiny commercial pot that can often be distracting, but here it does complement the stunning autumn colours of this maple.

It really is useful if you have your tree with you when selecting a pot because you can position possible alternatives in front of the tree, stand back and get a good idea of what it will look like.

Glazed or Unglazed?

In the past I have stood in a craft tent in the middle of a field and repotted an indoor tree from a blue pot into a green pot because the lady customer needed it to match her curtains in the lounge. This is not the criterion we should normally be using when deciding on the colour and finish of our next bonsai pot. Serious bonsai enthusiasts generally prefer unglazed pots, especially for conifers. Subtle-coloured glazes can be used with deciduous, flowering and fruiting trees, where the pot's appearance will match and complement the tree in the season when it is at its best. This may take into account the colour of flowers, the colour of fruit or the splendid array of tones and hues associated with spring or autumn foliage. Avoid strong glazes that are really gaudy and shining, as they tend to distract from the tree rather than com-

This Korean hornbeam in a Walsall Ceramics pot won best tree/pot combination at one of my Newstead exhibitions with a subtle glaze perfectly matching the bark colour.

plementing it. Commercial trees arriving from China and Japan are often found in brightly coloured pots and these do tend to appeal to the general public and first-time bonsai buyer.

Acquiring a few trees in such pots can add colour to a display and brighten up an area of the garden. However, once you become more experienced and involved in the hobby, as you acquire or develop a better-quality tree, you will realize and appreciate that the tree deserves a better, more appropriate pot. When it comes to choosing colour, if you are really unsure and can't decide, then if you select a pot where the colour is a reasonable match to the colour of the bark on the trunk, you won't go far wrong.

Students often ask my advice when purchasing a new pot and, contrary to what they will tell you, I do not always pick the most expensive one; some have even tried to confuse me by making sure they select potential pots that are all the same price! I will always try and point them in the right direction but, as I have said before, 'beauty is in the eye of the beholder'. You are the one who has to look at your tree every day, so it is vitally important that you are happy with what you see.

CHAPTER 10

YOUR BONSAI COLLECTION

Taking Stock

So what exactly are the signs that this bonsai bug has bitten, is becoming somewhat obsessive and gradually taking over your life? Your family will have already noticed that lengthy gaze at countless trees when you're out on a seemingly harmless day trip. The fact that they are looking down and all around them at activities, whilst you are staring upwards! The dog has never been as fit and every walk home is accompanied by some seedling sticking out of your pocket. Your patient partner has already observed the invading army of potential bonsai gradually taking over the herbaceous borders and conquering sections of the shrinking lawn. The patio, once the home of a barbecue and sun loungers, is now host to a tiered display structure where rampant bonsai battle for space. If this sounds like you, don't worry, it is perfectly normal!

As time goes by the issue of space does become a problem. Trees in training plant pots occupy every available inch in your garden and the display benches soon become overcrowded. Weeding and watering all these trees, especially in the summer, can take up most of your free time and leave you with very little time to actually work on your trees and enjoy them. They have all served their purpose, you have learned from them, practised your bonsai techniques on them and enjoyed them. As your knowledge and experience grow, your aspirations become greater and the standard of new trees or projects you acquire are generally

Your bonsai collection will rapidly take over every corner of the garden!

at a higher level. The moment will arrive when you literally do have to take stock of your collection and then you have to be ruthless.

Sentiment will play its part and it is hard to dispose of trees you have nurtured so carefully for many years, but now your bonsai time needs to be put to good use working on your best trees with the most potential. Trees that are struggling health-wise, those with serious flaws and trees that have limited potential in terms of further upward progress, are all candidates to be disposed of. You don't have to throw them in the compost bin or bonfire, maybe there are new bonsai beginners or gardening acquaintances in your neighbourhood who would be delighted with your cast-offs. As you progress further up the bonsai ladder, a tree you are happy to get rid of may become the star in someone else's bonsai collection. With this upward progression, what generally happens is that the number of trees in your collection becomes smaller but the quality becomes much higher. Better, more refined trees will take up more of your time in terms of ongoing maintenance but the satisfaction you get will be greater as you see your trees develop and realize their full potential.

Keeping Records

Taking photographs regularly and keeping accurate records are not only important but are worthwhile and can be extremely rewarding. You will be surprised how easy it is to forget just how far you have come with a tree. I look at some of my trees pictured in this book and take pride in their appearance, but then when I look at what I started with the difference is unbelievable. Taking pictures every year, especially deciduous trees in their winter image, is a good indication of how you are progressing with a tree and if your cultivation techniques are working.

Keeping records is also invaluable and today, like most things in life, applications can be acquired for your phone or computer to make the task easier. Many of my students have designed their own record sheets for each tree where they enter the details of acquisition, repotting dates, wiring/carving work, feeding schedules, pest treatment and dates/details of any pruning work carried out. Sometimes they read it back to me and it sounds like I am on trial in court: 'on the first of February 2012 you said...'. You will forget when you last repotted your trees, so having this information to hand is a big help when deciding which trees you need to repot each spring. When a tree responds really well to a feeding programme, pest treatment or the timing of specific pruning, it is imperative that you can look back and find out exactly what you did and when, because then you are in a position to repeat it.

A basic record sheet produced by The Yorkshire Bonsai Association.

Make a Plan

Having explained the benefits of keeping records and being able to look back, now we have to explore the merits of making plans and moving forwards. The winter is often a quieter time in the bonsai year, most trees are dormant and the demands of watering are much less onerous. This is a good time to update your records, take photographs and prepare for the next growing season. Which trees need to be repotted or checked in spring? Do any of them need new pots, which could be acquired during the winter months? Am I well stocked with bonsai compost and food for the season ahead?

In addition to planning major tasks, such as repotting, you should be assessing each tree for the year ahead. What are your objectives for each tree? What do you need to do to maintain the tree in good health or take the tree to its next higher level? Often, when students attend classes at the beginning of the growing season, we discuss each tree individually. I tell them which branches they have to let grow unchecked, which can be cut after a little growth, whilst some may have to be stopped almost immediately, as soon as new shoots emerge. Sometimes the timing of the pruning may be crucial to try to get the desired result, such as back-budding, for example. In this way they have a plan to follow for each tree that can then be broken down to give them a month by month schedule of work for the year ahead. The more trees you have, the more important this becomes, as the limited time you have available becomes more precious. This will help you prepare for busier and quieter times, helping you to allocate your workload accordingly. This planned approach is better than a haphazard wander in your garden each weekend just looking for a tree to have some fun with. If the tree develops well and you achieve your aim, then you know your techniques worked. If it's not turned out as well as you hoped, then you can look at what you did and contemplate changes for the next growing season.

Displaying/Showing Bonsai

In the Home

For the beginner with their first indoor bonsai, the tree is basically kept in the window where it grows. This is not a display, as such, but at least the tree can be enjoyed from the comfort of an easy chair. In the traditional Japanese home there is often found a tokonoma, which is like a recess or alcove used for artistic display. A bonsai would normally be accompanied by a scroll and a *kusamono* or accent plant. Such a display can be a deep source of contemplation or meditation, the three parts coming together to suggest a place or picture. For example, the bonsai itself or flowering grasses could indicate the time of year by their seasonal appearance, whilst a dragonfly on the scroll could suggest that the scene is near water. The possibilities are endless and whole books have been written on the display of bonsai alone.

If you have an alcove or a blank wall you can create a nice seasonal display. An outdoor tree can be brought inside for a few days when it is at its best to be enjoyed by you and your visitors. When I used to visit a bonsai friend in London, he would always bring one of his trees indoors and create a display especially for me and I really appreciated this.

A maple bonsai brought inside just to enjoy its vibrant spring colour.

With a blank wall and plain sheet you can create an impressive display indoors.

I installed this koi pond to complement my bonsai and Japanese garden elements.

In the Garden

I briefly mentioned in Chapter 5 about the merits of displaying your bonsai close to the house where the trees can enjoy an outdoor environment, whilst you can still get pleasure from your collection viewing it comfortably from indoors. Display benches can be constructed at varying heights on a patio or hard-standing, so that trees are easier to manage and can be viewed from a nearby window. Some enthusiasts will change an area of their garden to create a Japanese-themed section that will become home to their bonsai. Trees are often displayed on tall pillars at varying heights, using sawn telegraph poles, old railway sleepers, large timbers or brickwork topped with a concrete slab.

Such displays can transform a garden, enhance your collection as a whole and be marvelled at by friends and visitors. Granite lanterns, Japanese-style fencing, water bowls, trained cloud trees and neat gravelled areas can all

be incorporated into your garden feature. Many bonsai enthusiasts will often install a Japanese koi carp pond to accompany their bonsai, whilst many koi carp enthusiasts will display some bonsai around their pond. The two doctrines share many similarities, harmonize well together and are often found together in Japan.

In an Exhibition

As your trees develop and your bonsai skills improve, the time may come when you want to share the fruits of your labour with a wider audience. If you have joined a local bonsai group, then your first encounter with public display might be the annual club show. Some horticultural shows now include a bonsai section where trees are judged and awards presented. If the show scene appeals to you and your trees have reached a good standard, then you may be tempted to try and enter your

Japanese-style fencing, a granite Kasuga lantern and a sheltering dog!

tree in a national exhibition. It is better if you have already attended some of the larger bonsai events as a visitor, so that you know exactly what is expected of you and your trees.

Often you will have to submit photographs of your tree to the show organizers who will then decide if it is of the type and standard that they are looking for. If your aspirations are even greater, then you will find that there are international bonsai events held, which attract exhibitors and visitors from different countries. I have been very fortunate to have exhibited and won awards at both national and international events, as well as being involved in organizing such events. There is a lot of time and hard work involved, but I can assure you it is a very rewarding experience.

Exhibition Technique

If you decide to exhibit one of your trees, just remember it is not just a case of picking it up off your display bench and transporting it to the show venue. The tree is representing you, it showcases your skill and it tells people where you are in this hobby. Take great pride in your work, present it in the best possible way you can – eye-catching and immaculate. Prepare your tree in advance, as I mentioned in Chapter 8, where appearance has taken precedence over health to reach a high level of presentation in time for the exhibition.

The pot needs to be cleaned and oiled to get rid of the stains and dirt accumulated over the years. The soil needs to be mossed over to give the impression the tree is well established and has been in the pot a long time. Different mosses can be used, with coarser ones to the front and finer ones to the rear to give greater depth. Different shades of moss can be used to create light and dark areas and

I built four tokonomas like this one for my Newstead national bonsai exhibitions.

suggest movement, drawing the viewer into the composition. I would normally moss my trees at least three weeks before the exhibition to give it time to get established and enable me to make any repairs or adjustments, as required.

Any deadwood needs to be cleaned and bleached with lime sulphur to ensure that you get the exact colour and contrast you are looking for. With junipers and yew, you are looking for a stark-white finish to create that dramatic contrast with the green foliage and rich, orange/red bark. With deciduous trees and pines, you are trying for a more subtle and natural-looking, silvery grey finish. The basic lime sulphur can be changed in colour by adding black or white poster paints. I have also known people use ink, tea, coffee and other 'secret' ingredients to try to achieve the desired effect. Once again, this job is best done a few weeks prior to the exhibition, so that you can see how it dries and if it needs to be reapplied.

The bark on the trunk and main branches also needs to be cleaned. A nylon brush or old toothbrush with a little warm soapy water is ideal. With juniper, yew and cypress trees you are removing the dark, dirty flaky bark to reveal the bright orange/red/brown colour hidden below. With pines and older deciduous trees, the flaky mature bark is

part of its character and age. We want to retain this, so any cleaning here to remove dirt or moss growth must be done very lightly so as not to disturb the flaky bark itself.

It goes without saying that the foliage mass creating the overall image of the tree simply has to be pristine. Open spaces have to be clearly defined with neat, uninterrupted lines. Any foliage hanging below branch lines is removed. Spaces may have to be created in dense clouds of foliage to give a lighter, more natural appearance. The tree should have a well-balanced, uniform appearance, with the foliage evenly distributed throughout the canopy. I have often been up into the early hours preparing trees for exhibitions, removing fine shoots and twigs before progressing to individual leaves in order to achieve that immensely satisfying, final image. You will know when you get it right because you won't be able to walk past the tree without stopping for a few moments in awe, to savour all its glory and, when you feel like this, visitors to the exhibition will react in exactly the same way.

Any major bonsai exhibition today will expect you to exhibit your tree on a suitable bonsai table. Some people have made a business out of this and can supply a bespoke table for your tree based on recognized Japanese styles, but these do not come cheap. Many would-be carpenters have challenged themselves to make their own table and have come up with some surprisingly good results. As a last resort, you may be able to improvise with a simple wooden plinth, bamboo slats or some form of matting, but you will need to clarify acceptance of this with the show's organizers. Some shows will allocate you a space and encourage you to be creative, to form a display that can include a scroll and other accompaniments, such as a *kusamono*. Everything in your display should be presented to the same high standard as your tree. They should complement and enhance your tree and not detract from it in any way.

Exhibiting your trees can be good for you and good for your trees; it makes you do the work required. When I organized my national Newstead Bonsai Extravaganza every two years, naturally most of my students wanted to participate, but with show entries coming from Scotland and Wales, as well as throughout England, the standard was very high. The show gave my students something to aim for, something to aspire to; it was an end-product that drove them to work on good trees and to take their material to as high a level as possible in the time available. A challenge like this can bring the best out of the hobby, the best out of your trees and, more importantly, the best out of you!

One moment in time....A Work in Progress...... By John Hanby

My Korean juniper, part of a work in progress section in one of my Newstead exhibitions but still presented to a good standard.

GLOSSARY

Akadama This bonsai potting medium is a naturally occurring clay-like substance graded into different-sized particles and imported already bagged from Japan.

Contact spray A contact pesticide is designed to exterminate pests directly on contact.

Foliage clouds The shallow-arched mass of leaves at the middle/ends of branches.

Grafting One plant's tissue (part of the stem) is added to the tissue of another (root stock) for growing specific varieties that will then mature more quickly.

Growing season The period of time when plants grow, which is usually between spring and autumn.

Internode The distance between two nodes.

Jin When we strip the bark off a branch or pruned stub to create deadwood, it is referred to by the Japanese term as a jin.

Kusamono A potted arrangement of wild grasses and flowers displayed alongside bonsai.

Nebari This refers to the flare and exposed roots at the base of the trunk, which give the bonsai a more natural, well-balanced and older appearance.

Node The joint between a leaf and the stem where new buds will emerge.

Raw material A tree or shrub in its natural-grown state prior to any pruning, wiring or styling to create the basis for a bonsai.

Shari If a strip of bark is removed from a section of the trunk, then this is referred to as a shari. In nature, when a substantial branch or major root dies, the vein of bark linking the two can dieback on the trunk creating a natural shari.

Systemic pesticide A pesticide that is absorbed into a plant and distributed throughout its tissues.

Tap root The main, dominant, large root growing vertically downwards from which other roots sprout.

Tokonoma An alcove or recess in the Japanese home used for artistic display.

Turnbuckle Two threaded bolts screwed into a metal frame for gradually tensioning cables.

Yamadori A tree collected from the wild.

FURTHER INFORMATION

Further Reading

Adams, Peter, *Bonsai with Japanese Maples*
(Timber Press, 2006)
Barton, Dan, *The Bonsai Book* (Random House, 1994)
Chan, Peter, *The Bonsai Beginners Bible*
(Mitchell Beazley, 2018)
Cousins, Craig, *Totally Bonsai* (Tuttle Publishing, 2016)
Lewis, Colin, *Bonsai Basics* (Aura, 2002)
Norman, Ken, *The Complete Practical Encyclopaedia of
Bonsai* (Lorenz, 2016)
Prescott, David, *The Bonsai Handbook*
(IMM Lifestyle, 2015)
Qing Quan, Zhao and Kempinski, Rob, *Penjing: The
Chinese Art of Bonsai*
(Betterlink Press Incorporated, 2012)
Tomlinson, Harry, *101 Essential Tips Bonsai*
(Dorling Kindersley Ltd, 2019)

Useful Websites

www.bonsaiempire.com
Bonsai community and online courses
www.bonsaifocus.com International bonsai magazine
www.bonsaiplaza.com Online shop
www.fobbsbonsai.co.uk Federation of British Bonsai
Societies
www.johnhanbybonsai.co.uk Bonsai tuition, seasonal
maintenance, blog and shop
www.kaizenbonsai.com Online shop and blog
www.mendipbonsai.co.uk Bonsai tuition and sales
www.scottishbonsai.org Scottish Bonsai Association
www.stonelantern.com Online shop and blog
www.ukbonsaiassoc.org National bonsai association and
information
www.wbffbonsai.com World Bonsai Friendship Federation

Bonsai Nurseries

England

Cambridgeshire
Banksia Bonsai, Chapel Lane, South Brink, Wisbech,
Cambridgeshire PE14 0RX

Kent
LV Bonsai, 2 Taunton Close, Barnehurst, Bexleyheath,
Kent DA7 6NN

Northumberland
Willowbog Bonsai, Willowbog Farm, Wark, Hexham,
Northumberland NE48 3EF

Nottinghamshire
Greenwood Bonsai Studio, Ollerton Road, Arnold,
Nottingham NG5 8PR

South Yorkshire
All Things Bonsai, Godfreys Garden Centre, Hardwick
Lane, Sheffield, South Yorkshire S26 2BE

Surrey
Herons Bonsai, Wiremill Lane, Newchapel, Near Lingfield,
Surrey RH7 6HJ
The Bonsai Shed, Hill Park Rose Nurseries, Woodstock
Lane North, Thames Ditton, Surrey KT6 5HN
Windybank Bonsai, 60 Woodmansterne Lane, Carshalton,
Surrey SM5 4BJ

Scotland

Lanarkshire
Wattston Bonsai, 104 Greengairs Road, Airdrie,
Lanarkshire ML6 7SY

Bonsai Potters

Tony Remington www.bonsaipotsuk.com
Steve Kitchman www.chinamist.co.uk
Dan Barton www.danbartonbonsaipots.wordpress.com
Victor Harris www.erinbonsai.com
Andy Pearson www.stonemonkeyceramics.co.uk
David Jones www.walsall-studio-ceramics.co.uk
Ian Baillie can be found on Facebook by searching 'Bonsai
Pots by Ian Baillie'

ACKNOWLEDGEMENTS

Photography

With the exception of the following all photographs were taken by the author. Photographs taken by Daniel Lyons: page 14; page 17 (bottom); page 172 (all); page 188; page 189. Photographs taken by David Hill: page 15 (Satsuki azalea); page 171 (bottom). Photographs taken by Roy Hicks: page 32 (all); page 134, top right. Photograph taken by Susan Harston: page 85 (bottom). Photographs taken from Pixabay: page 6, page 163 (top). Photographer unknown: page 25.

General

Many thanks to the following students and clients for their continued support and for allowing their trees to appear in this book: Derek Bacon, Henry Barber, Keith Beckett, Allan Bentley, Rob Brown, Paul Bryant, Paul Cawthorn, Stan Collinge, Michelle Crowther, Paul Dixon, Tomas Eibner, Ian Flaxman, Brian Glover, Simon Gueller, Kevin and Debbie Hale, Bob Harrison, Susan Harston, Andrew Harwood, Neil Hay, Roy Hicks, Duncan Hield, Glyn Holmes, Richard Houghton, Andrew Jones, Kevin Malone, Lee Maloney, Peter Marshall, John Midgley, Judith Milner, Matthew Moorhouse, Alison Mortimer, David Peel, Richard Pope, Lyn and Steve Puffer, Alan Rhodes, Kevin Richardson, Scott Ripley, Mike Rose, Shane Ryan, Chris Skinner, Paul Taylor, Ian Wilman, and Oliver Wiper.

We have made every attempt to contact the present owners of trees featured in this book and apologize for any omissions.

Special thanks to the late Harry Tomlinson, to Dan Barton and to Danny Use for their encouragement, inspiration and friendship.

INDEX